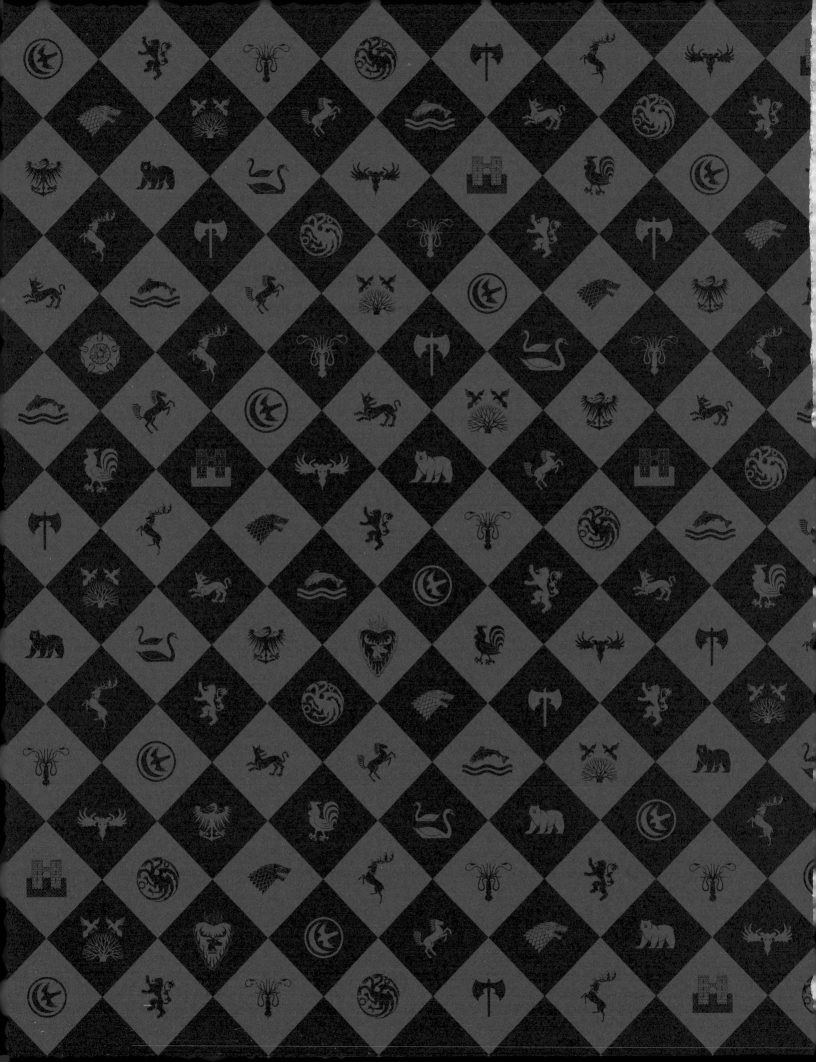

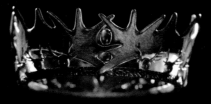

INSIDE HBO'S

GAME OF THRONES™

BRYAN COGMAN

Preface by GEORGE R. R. MARTIN ♦ *Foreword by* DAVID BENIOFF & D. B. WEISS

CHRONICLE BOOKS

Acknowledgments

Working on this extraordinary series with such passionate and gifted people—the phrase "dream come true" doesn't do it justice. So thanks first to David Benioff and D. B. Weiss, my bosses, mentors, and friends, who gave me the incredible opportunity not only to write for *Game of Thrones* but also to put together this special book. And, of course, thanks to George R. R. Martin for creating these fantastic worlds and vivid characters—my continual hope is that we do his books proud.

Thanks also to Gemma Jackson, Michele Clapton, and all the *GoT* cast and crew, past and present, who graciously took the time (in the midst of a hectic season two production schedule) to share their thoughts on the show. And apologies to those interviewed who didn't make it into the book—we had only so much space!

Thanks to co-producer Greg Spence, postproduction coordinator Martin Mahon, concept artists Ashleigh Jeffers and Kim Pope, art department coordinator Joanne Hall, and unit photographer Helen Sloan for their invaluable help in gathering the art for this book. And a big, big, big thank you to Lucy Caird, the book would have been nearly impossible, if not for her heroic work in scheduling the cast and crew interviews.

Finally, my undying gratitude to my wife, Mandy, for her enduring patience, counsel, and love.

—Bryan Cogman

Special thanks to James Costos, Stacey Abiraj, Josh Goodstadt, Janis Fein, Cara Grabowski, Robin Eisgrau, and Vicky Lavergne.

Game of Thrones series photographs by Nick Briggs, Ashleigh Jeffers, Paul Schiraldi, Helen Sloan, and Oliver Upton.

Costume illustrations by Michele Clapton and Kimberly Pope.

Concept art by Julian Caldow, Marc Homes, Gavin Jones, Tobias Mannewitz, Kimberly Pope, and William Simpson.

www.hbo.com

Copyright © 2012 by HOME BOX OFFICE, INC.

Library of Congress Cataloging-in-Publication data available under ISBN 978-1-4521-1010-3

Manufactured in China

Designed by HEADCASE DESIGN (Paul Kepple *and* Ralph Geroni)

10 9 8 7 6 5 4 3 2 1

CHRONICLE BOOKS

680 Second Street ♦ San Francisco, California 94107 ♦ www.chroniclebooks.com

Table of Contents

PREFACE: FROM PAGE TO SCREEN

BY GEORGE R. R. MARTIN

George R. R. Martin on the Game of Thrones *set in Belfast.*

David Benioff and D. B. Weiss are brave men or mad men. They'd have to be to take on a job like bringing *A Game of Thrones* (and the rest of my massive epic fantasy series *A Song of Ice and Fire*) to television.

There is no more hazardous task in Hollywood than trying to make a popular or critically acclaimed book into a television series or feature film. Hollywood Boulevard is lined with the skulls and bleached bones of all those who have tried and failed . . . and for every known failure, there are a hundred you have never heard of, because the adaptations were abandoned somewhere along the way, often after years of development and dozens of scripts.

Now, a story is a story is a story, but each medium has its own way of telling that story. A film, a television show, a book, a comic, each has its own strengths and weaknesses, things it does well, things it does poorly, things that it can hardly do at all.

Moving from page to screen is never easy.

A novelist has techniques and devices at his command that are not available to the scriptwriter: internal dialogue, unreliable narrators, first-person and tight third-person points of view, flashbacks, expository narrative, and a host of others. As a novelist, I strive to put my readers inside the heads of my characters, make them privy to their thoughts, let them see the world through their eyes. But the camera stands outside the character, so the viewpoint is of necessity external rather than internal. Aside from voice-overs (always an intrusion, I think, a crutch at best), the scriptwriter must depend on the director and the cast to convey the depths of emotion, subtleties of thought, and contradictions of character that a novelist can simply tell the reader about in clear, straightforward prose.

There are certain practical challenges as well. A television drama has a running time of sixty minutes (for premium cable) or about forty-five minutes (for a network show). There's more flexibility with a feature film, but even there, you had best come in around two hours. Go over three hours, and the studios are certain to start cutting. But most novels simply have too much story for these time frames. Produce a direct scene-for-scene, line-for-line adaptation, and you'll end up with something too long for either flatscreen or Cineplex. And the problem is compounded when your source material is an epic fantasy. *Lord of the Rings* was broken into three volumes because the book that Tolkien delivered was three times as long as most novels published in the 1950s. And my own books, like almost all contemporary fantasies, are a deal longer than Tolkien's.

Budget and shooting schedules also have a major impact on what can and cannot be done when moving from page to screen. It is easy for someone like me to write of a stupendous feasting hall with a hundred hearths, large enough to seat a thousand knights, each in his own heraldic finery. But pity the poor producers who have to reproduce that on screen. First, they have to build this gigantic set, with all those hearths ("Do we really need a hundred? Could we have, say, six?"). Then they have to find a thousand extras to fill those benches. Then they have to set the costume designer to work sketching out a thousand heraldic surcoats, after which they need to fit the extras and sew the costumes and . . . well, you get the idea. Alternatively, the producers can try to do it all with CGI. A wonderful resource, CGI, but that's costly and time-consuming as well. And the budget is the budget, whether it is one million dollars or one hundred million.

Over the course of my career, I've worked both sides of the great divide between page and screen. When I first broke into print in the early 1970s, it was as a novelist and short story writer, working exclusively with prose. By the 1980s, some producers and studios had noticed me, and I had my first experiences with my work being optioned, adapted, and (in a couple of cases) even filmed. I started writing scripts myself in the middle of that decade, initially for the CBS revival of *The Twilight Zone*, and I found myself adapting stories by other writers. I went on to work for three years as a writer/producer on the television series *Beauty and the Beast*, and then for five years in development (more commonly known as "development hell"), writing television pilots and feature films, most of which were never made.

All told, I spent the best part of a decade in Hollywood. I think I did some good work, but coming from the world of prose, as I did, I was constantly smashing up against the walls of what was possible in film and television. "George, this is great," the studio would say, whenever I turned in the first draft of a new script, "but it would cost five times our budget to shoot what's on the page. You need to lose ten pages . . . cut twelve characters . . . turn this huge battle

whole imaginary world and a cast of thousands. Absolutely unfilmable, of course. No studio or network would ever touch a story like this, I knew. These would be good books, maybe great books, but that was all they'd ever be. (Ah, the irony . . .)

It was about the time *A Clash of Kings* was published that we first began to hear from producers and screenwriters interested in optioning the series (*Clash* was the second volume but the first to hit the bestseller lists). I was skeptical. My agents and I fielded a few phone calls, took a few meetings, listened to the proposals . . . but I remained dubious. They were all talking about doing *A Song of Ice and Fire*—all of it, all seven books, including the ones I had not written yet—as a feature film. No doubt they were inspired by the huge success of Peter Jackson's *Lord of the Rings* films and hoped to duplicate that. I had been inspired by Jackson's work as well, but I knew the same approach would never work for my own fantasies. My series was too big, too

when it came to producing quality, adult television. But it couldn't be as a movie-for-television or even a miniseries. It would have to be a full-on series, with an entire season devoted to each novel. The only problem was, HBO had never done fantasy nor shown any interest in the genre. It would never happen.

And then I met David Benioff and Dan Weiss, at a lunch set up by my agent Vince Gerardis at the Palm in Los Angeles. It started as a lunch and ended after dinner, and it turned out that David and Dan had the same dream I did, of doing *A Song of Ice and Fire* as a series on HBO. "You're mad," I told them. "It's too big. It's too complicated. It's too expensive. HBO doesn't do fantasy."

The two madmen were undeterred. They loved the story and were convinced that they could bring it to the screen. So I let them try.

Best call I ever made.

As I write, the first season of *Game of Thrones* has come and gone, to great popular and critical acclaim, including Emmy® and Golden Globe® nominations, and wins for Peter Dinklage for his performance as Tyrion Lannister. Writers, producers, directors, costumers, special effects designers, stuntmen, and many more have been recognized for their outstanding work by their peers. Filming on the second season has been completed, and the new episodes are now in post. And the series and the books alike have become a part of our cultural zeitgeist, with references and tips of the hat from other shows as diverse as *The Simpsons*, *The Big Bang Theory*, *Parks and Recreation*, *Castle*, and *Chuck*.

"You're mad," I told them. "It's too big. It's too complicated. It's too expensive."

---

scene into a duel . . . get down from twelve matte paintings to two. . . ." Et cetera.

And I would. That was the job. But I always preferred those early, unproduceable first drafts of mine to the final shooting scripts, and after ten years in the industry, I was tired of reining myself in. It was that, as much as anything else, that led me to return to prose, my first love, in the 1990s. The result was *A Game of Thrones* and its sequels (five books published to date, two more planned and on the way). I had spent years pitching, writing, and developing concepts for television, all eminently doable for TV budgets. Now I wanted to put all that behind me, to pull out all the stops. Huge castles, vast dramatic landscapes, deserts and mountains and swamps, dragons, direwolves, gigantic battles with thousands to a side, glittering armor, gorgeous heraldry, swordfights and tournaments, characters who were complicated, conflicted, flawed, a

complex. Just one of my volumes was as long as all three of Professor Tolkien's. It took three films to do justice to the *Lord of the Rings*. It would take twenty to do *A Song of Ice and Fire*, and there wasn't a studio in the world mad enough to commit to that.

Still, the conversations did get me thinking about how my story could possibly be brought from page to screen. Television was the only way to go, I realized. Not a network series; that would never fly. Network budgets were simply not high enough, and their censors would choke on all the sex and violence in the novels. At best you'd get bowdlerized versions, weak tea instead of strong mead. A long miniseries might work, something on the order of *Roots* or *Shogun*, but the networks weren't making those kinds of epic minis anymore.

It would have to be HBO, I decided. The people who'd made *The Sopranos*, *Deadwood*, *Rome*. No one else even came close

No one is more pleased or astonished than I am. Pretty damn good for a story that I was once convinced could never make that jump from page to screen.

How did they do it, you ask?

Bryan Cogman has been part of this journey from the very beginning. He was the first person David and Dan hired when they got the green light, and he's lived most of the last few years in Westeros. I'll let him tell you.

Like David and Dan, he knew this job was dangerous when he took it.

— **GEORGE R. R. MARTIN**
Santa Fe, New Mexico
January 27, 2012

FOREWORD

Seven Questions with David Benioff & D. B. Weiss

As executive producers and head writers, David Benioff and D. B. (Dan) Weiss share the helm on Game of Thrones. They became friends some sixteen years ago when they met while studying Irish literature at Trinity College in Dublin. In the years that followed, they each achieved success as novelists and feature-film screenwriters, but they hadn't found a good project to collaborate on until they came across George R. R. Martin's epic fantasy saga A Song of Ice and Fire.

BRYAN COGMAN: *What was your first encounter with George R. R. Martin's books?*

D. B. WEISS: I first encountered the books as a truly massive stack of paper sitting on the floor beside David's front door. They literally looked like a doorstop.

DAVID BENIOFF: In January 2006, I spoke on the phone with a literary agent who told me about some of the books he represented. One, in particular, sounded interesting: *A Game of Thrones* by George R. R. Martin. I'll confess that I hadn't heard of the book, or of George, before this phone call. I had been a massive fan of fantasy fiction when I was younger, particularly high fantasy, but after reading one Tolkien rip-off too many, I lost my taste for it. Still, hearing about the novel intrigued me, so I said I'd be curious to read the book. A few days later a package arrived at my doorstep. A heavy package, containing the first four books of *A Song of Ice and Fire*, more than four thousand pages in total, each sporting traditional high fantasy covers—bearded men wielding swords, distant castles, sexy sorceresses with impressive cleavage. I thought, "Well, this looks like your standard sort of thing." Within a few pages I knew I was wrong. After Jaime Lannister pushed Bran Stark from a high window, I was addicted. A couple of hundred pages later, I called Dan, one of my oldest friends and someone I knew was once as obsessed with fantasy as I had been. Both of us had been proud dungeon masters in our respective Dungeons and Dragons games. Okay, maybe "proud" is too strong a word.

D. B. Weiss and David Benioff

Maybe we didn't exactly brag about those D&D games at high school parties. But still.

D. B. WEISS: He asked me to check out *A Game of Thrones* to make sure he wasn't crazy. I checked it out, had a similar "holy shit" reaction to Bran going out the window, and three days later I'd read nine hundred pages. I hadn't read a book that way since I was twelve. It was a powerful reading experience. Compulsive. Propulsive.

DAVID BENIOFF: Convulsive.

D. B. WEISS: At times.

BRYAN COGMAN: *What made you want to adapt the material, and why did you do so for HBO television as opposed to a feature film?*

DAVID BENIOFF: You don't enter into any adaptation process lightly. In the case of *Game of Thrones*, we've dedicated six years of our lives to the show. We did it for a simple reason that will be familiar to George's readers: We fell in love with the books. We fell in love with the world he created, with the sprawl of Westeros and Essos. We fell in love with the characters, hundreds of them, the good as well as the bad, with the Starks and the Lannisters and the Targaryens and the Greyjoys. We fell in love with the brutality of the narrative: No one is ever safe. Good does not triumph over evil. Awful people have sympathetic traits and lovable people have loathsome traits.

D. B. WEISS: If a large part of your livelihood is adapting source material for the screen, you're always on the lookout for deep characters, a beautifully crafted and compelling story, passion, violence, intrigue, humanity, and all the ambiguities that come with a fully realized world . . . and you never find them all in the same place. Except we did. It was exhilarating and terrifying.

DAVID BENIOFF: And all of the things we loved made it impossible to consider the books as source material for feature films. First off, compressing each book into a two-hour movie would mean discarding dozens of subplots and scores of characters. Second, a fantasy movie of this scope, financed by a major studio, would almost certainly need a PG-13 rating. That means no sex, no blood, no profanity. Fuck that.

BRYAN COGMAN: *Describe some of the challenges of adapting such a sprawling narrative, with so many characters and plot threads.*

D. B. WEISS: The question answers itself: there is a lot in there. George hasn't just told a story—he's built a world. Ten hours is a fair amount of time to tell a story, but to establish a world, you have to be efficient or risk losing things you love. In the first season, I'd say we managed to keep almost everything we really loved. Going forward, alas, there will have to be some sacrifices or compressions—otherwise we'd need thirty episodes per season, and our casting budget would sink the ship. But the aim will always be to preserve the spirit of the series—to make a show that makes viewers feel the way the books made us feel when we first read them . . . and reread them, and re-reread them.

BRYAN COGMAN: *Which scenes or particular lines of dialogue are you most proud of writing?*

DAVID BENIOFF: The bit where Syrio tells Arya about his beliefs: "There is only one god. His name is Death. And there is only one thing to say to Death. Not today."

That scene [from Episode 106] perfectly showcases the collaborative process on *Game of Thrones*. George, of course, invented both Arya and Syrio. We originally didn't plan to have this particular Arya-Syrio scene in the episode, but [Episode 106 cowriter] Jane Espenson convinced us it was a good idea. Dan took Jane's original scene and reconfigured it. I came up with those lines about Death. Miltos Yerolemou [who played Syrio] took some dialogue that could have sounded portentous or pretentious, or portentously pretentious, and delivered it just so. And Dan Minahan directed a perfect little scene.

D. B. WEISS: They're pretty simple, but the lines I'm most proud of are probably in the scene between Robert and Cersei [in Episode 105], when they're having a rare moment of clarity about their toxic swamp of a marriage. Cersei asks Robert if there was ever a chance for them to be happy together, and Robert tells her the truth: "No." Then he asks her, "Does that make you feel better or worse?" And she tells him, "It doesn't make me feel anything."

It doesn't look like much on the page, really. So let me amend the question to "What are the lines you're most proud of having actors deliver with devastating effectiveness?"

DAVID BENIOFF: You, sir, are mistaken. The best line you wrote has to be when Sam says, "I always wanted to be a wizard."

BRYAN COGMAN: *Which of the story's many themes resonate most with you?*

DAVID BENIOFF: In the real world, terrible shit happens to good people and duplicitous assholes often enjoy tremendous success. So how come in fantasy worlds good always triumphs and evil suffers resounding defeat? It sounds odd to say about a story featuring dragons and ice demons and silver-haired princesses, but George brought a measure of harsh realism to high fantasy. He introduced gray tones into a black-and-white universe.

D. B. WEISS: I always thought of it as a story about power, first and foremost. Who wants it, why they want it, how they get it, what they do with it, what it costs them and their families. It's a theme that swirls through many great epic stories, from *The Iliad* to *The Godfather* to *Lord of the Rings*. And in that vein, it's also a story about the ways the personal becomes the political, the way individual loves and lusts and hates and regrets can have repercussions that stretch far beyond the people they affect immediately.

BRYAN COGMAN: *Why was Northern Ireland the ultimate choice for the bulk of the shoot and the* Game of Thrones *base of operations?*

DAVID BENIOFF: A number of reasons: Northern Ireland offers a broad array of diverse locations within a short drive. Windswept hilltops, stony beaches, lush meadows, high cliffs, bucolic streams—we can shoot a day at any of these places and still sleep that night in Belfast. And Belfast is a wonderful base, a small city where we've felt at home right from the beginning. Our local crew is stocked with remarkably passionate, talented folks. Unlike some places where big productions are commonplace, like Hollywood or London, we still feel a sense of excitement from the community that we've chosen Belfast as the show's hub.

BRYAN COGMAN: *Finally, at what point did you realize [former assistant, now story editor] Bryan Cogman was the key to the success of this thing?*

D. B. WEISS: Sadly, it was moments after we fired him and sold his baby to the circus.

DAVID BENIOFF: He constantly threatened to quit our show and work on *Camelot*. True story.

1 The Wall

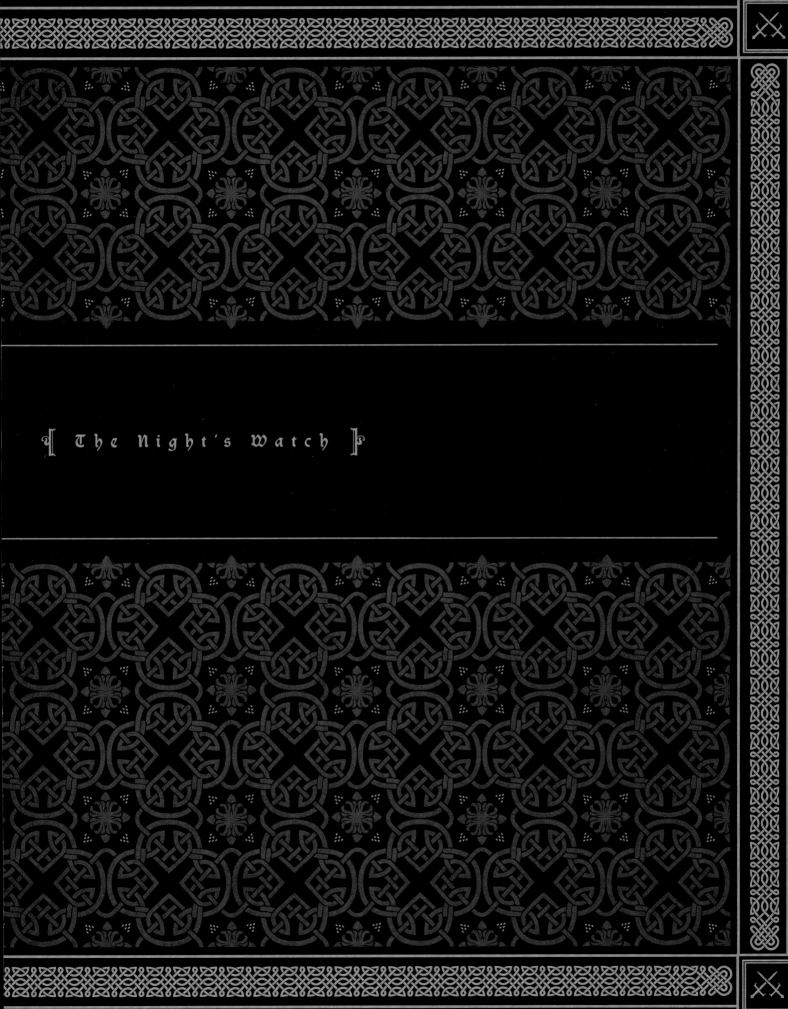

{ [The Night's Watch] }

he seed (for the Wall) was books, when I visited the UK The sun was going down, and autumn, a chilly day. The wind

I tried to imagine what it would be like to be a Roman legionary stationed on that wall, someone from Italy or Africa; they had soldiers from all over the world at that point. You're standing there, essentially at the end of the world, and you could see hills and forests beyond. What enemy is going to come out of those woods? What is going to emerge and attack you from

planted ten years before I started writing the

for the first time and went to Hadrian's Wall.

I stood on top of the wall, looking north. It was

was blowing, and it awoke something in me.

eyond the wall? It was a really profound moment, and
t touched something in my imagination. There was a
tory there. Of course, on Hadrian's Wall, what would
ave emerged from those woods would be Scotsman!
had to do better than a Scotsman. And fantasy is
nevitably bigger, so I knew the Wall had to be bigger.

— GEORGE R. R. MARTIN
(executive producer, author of A Song of Ice and Fire*)*

WHITE WALKERS

A BRIEF HISTORY

"Oh, my sweet summer child, what do you know about fear?
Fear is for the winter, when the snows fall a hundred feet deep.
Fear is for the Long Night . . . when the White Walkers
move through the woods."

—Old Nan

Thousands of years ago, according to legend, a brutal winter and a horrific darkness engulfed the whole of Westeros. This darkness—known as the Long Night—lasted a generation. It was the time of the White Walkers, demonic creatures born from the icy wastelands of the far North.

Leading monstrous armies of the dead, the White Walkers waged war against the living, sweeping over villages, holdfasts, and cities, utterly destroying everything in their wake.

Eventually, an alliance of the First Men and the Children of the Forest brought the Long Night to an end. Together, they defeated the White Walkers, driving them back into the uncharted reaches of the far North. To keep them from ever invading again, the peoples of Westeros built the Wall, and they set upon it the Night's Watch. For a millennium, the White Walkers have not been seen, and so they have become more myth than real, a bedtime story to frighten disobedient children. But as disturbing accounts arrive from beyond the Wall, some wonder if the White Walkers have returned . . . and are preparing to strike again.

[ABOVE] *Early concept art, White Walker.* ✤ [OPPOSITE] *The Haunted Forest, where wildlings and worse dwell.* ✤ [PREVIOUS SPREAD] *The Wall.* ✤ [PAGE 11] *The rangers venture north.*

THE PROLOGUE

EPISODE 101: "WINTER IS COMING"

IN THE OPENING MOMENTS OF GAME OF THRONES, THREE MEN OF THE NIGHT'S WATCH—SER WAYMAR ROYCE, WILL, AND GARED—VENTURE BEYOND THE WALL. THEIR ROUTINE RANGING MISSION TURNS DEADLY WHEN THEY ENCOUNTER THE LEGENDARY AND HORRIFIC WHITE WALKERS, AND ONLY WILL (PLAYED BY BRONSON WEBB) ESCAPES WITH HIS LIFE.

WILL SIMPSON *(storyboard artist)*: I was talking over the first storyboard for the sequence with [director] Tim Van Patten. Tim described it very specifically—all this great atmosphere and mood. It was a really nice way to open the series, hitting the audience with something abstract, something they've never seen before, and throwing them into the story.

TIM VAN PATTEN *(director, season one)*: The look of the White Walkers was the first challenge. At the last minute, we finally arrived with the look that exists, but not before every small detail was discussed at length. How would they have adapted to their surroundings? Skin tone? Features? Height? How would they move? Their wardrobe? Weapons?

WILL SIMPSON: I did three paintings of the White Walkers during the production of the original pilot, very early concepts. The original idea came from the description in the book—the idea that they're meant to be these frozen entities.

ADAM McINNES *(VFX supervisor, season one)*: When Tim Van Patten storyboarded the White Walker prologue sequence, the presence of the creatures was far more extensive than was ultimately used in the show. This was good for a number of reasons. It meant we were all pushed to find the best affordable solution for the crea-

"I saw what I saw . . . I saw the White Walkers."

{ Will }

[above] *Night's Watch rangers Gared (Dermot Keaney) and Ser Waymar Royce (Rob Ostlere) search the woods.* ◆ [opposite] *Bronson Webb as Will, an ill-fated ranger of the Night's Watch.*

tures without just avoiding seeing them from the outset. Ultimately, we decided the Walkers would be played by actors in suits, made up to look inhuman. Conor O'Sullivan, our prosthetics specialist, commissioned some concept art to sell the idea.

ALIK SAKHAROV *(director of photography, season one)*: I've known Tim Van Patten since 1998, when we worked on the first season of *The Sopranos*, so we've developed a shorthand over the years. He and I spent a week in his apartment—drinking great wine and eating a lot of pasta, naturally—and we shot ideas back and forth. We'd pore over the script line by line, look at the location photos, and imagine what the action would be. I remember we paced it out in his apartment, each move of the rangers, acting it out almost like theater, a black box technique. Then we proceeded to break the sequence down into shots—starting with Will riding along, an extreme wide shot first. Do we pan or do we track along with him? Details like that you discuss ad nauseam because, depending on what kind of shot you use, you inspire a different emotional response in the viewer. For me, the key to that first sequence was the deliberate pace, and Timmy's a master of timing.

ADAM McINNES: The actors in the Walker suits had to move as best they could in difficult terrain with minimal sight, since the masks reduced vision to a

WILL SIMPSON: The interesting thing with this sequence is that I went out to the actual location [Tollymore Forest in Northern Ireland] with Tim and Alik and took notes, scribbling away as they discussed it. I was seeing it all there, right in front of me, before drawing it, which doesn't usually happen. Tim was superb to work with, very collaborative. I worked hard at getting real movement and energy into the boards to help him realize the sequence.

pinhole. We added the blue glow to the eyes in post-production.

TIM VAN PATTEN: We ended up changing the sequence from night, the way it was scripted, to dusk in order to better control the shots and feel more of the environment. We filmed deep in the forest, which presented further challenges, and our special effects guys had to create all the snow.

It took about three days total—none of it easy, but all of it satisfying.

WILL SIMPSON: What I love about that prologue is you start with this crazy sequence basically a horror movie, and then you don't see the Walkers again for the whole season! But it's always, as a viewer, in the back of your mind, just as it is for the guys on the Wall. ❧

[left] *On location in Tollymore Forest.* ♦ [top] *The White Walkers are ready for "action."* ♦ [above bottom] *A grisly discovery beyond the Wall.* ♦ [opposite top] *Concept art, the Wall.* ♦ [opposite bottom] *Director Tim Van Patten references storyboards on set.*

THE NIGHT'S WATCH
A BRIEF HISTORY

*"Night gathers, and now my watch begins. ✧ It shall not end until my death.
I shall take no wife, hold no lands, father no children. ✧ I shall wear no crowns
and win no glory. ✧ I shall live and die at my post. ✧ I am the sword in the darkness.
I am the watcher on the walls. ✧ I am the shield that guards the realms of men.
I pledge my life and honor to the Night's Watch, for this night and all the nights to come."*

—The Night's Watch oath

The Night's Watch is a sworn brotherhood dedicated to defending the realms of men against the return of the White Walkers and from other dark forces that lurk in the far North. Their post is the mighty Wall, a massive fortification of ice and stone some seven hundred feet high that was erected by the First Men in the wake of the Long Night. This fabled structure, unlike any ever built, stretches from one end of Westeros to the other, its entire length guarded and maintained by the men of the Watch.

A man of the Night's Watch wears no sigil; he is garbed entirely in black and often referred to as a "black brother." He swears an oath of lifelong service; his only allegiance is to his fellow men of the Watch. He forsakes his family name and any lands or titles; his past is forgotten, washed away. A black brother must remain celibate, unmarried, childless, for the founders of the Night's Watch believed that love is the death of duty. Promising a life of hardship and great sacrifice, the Night's Watch oath must not be taken lightly—the punishment for desertion is death. Yet at the Wall, class distinctions are left behind as proud volunteers from noble houses stand side by side with petty thieves conscripted from dungeons. Anyone can rise up in the ranks; a man gets what he earns on the Wall.

Despite the long disappearance of the White Walkers, the Night's Watch has another formidable enemy to contend with. For generations, seminomadic barbarians known as "wildlings" have menaced the people of the North. Styling themselves as "freefolk," they refuse to be bound by the laws and customs of the Seven Kingdoms. Occasionally throughout history, the different wildling clans have rallied behind a single leader, a "King-Beyond-the-Wall," and attempted large-scale attacks against the realm. Each time these have been soundly defeated, thanks to the courageous men of the Night's Watch. But now a new wildling king, called Mance Rayder, has united the wildlings with a fervor not seen in more than a hundred years.

At the height of its glory, the Watch commanded great respect throughout the land, but service as a black brother no longer carries the prestige it once did. House Stark and other houses in the northern regions continue to recognize its importance for the safety and stability of the realm, but the powerful houses of the southern kingdoms do not share this view. These houses don't regard the wildlings as a serious threat, and they don't believe the White Walkers will return—if they ever existed. They believe the Night's Watch is a misguided, obsolete order comprised of useless outcasts, criminals, and ne'er-do-wells. As such, the Watch's numbers have steadily dwindled to less than a thousand, and only three of the nineteen castles along the Wall are functional. But, in spite of these hardships, the black brothers continue to stand their lonely vigil.

[ABOVE] *Jon Snow (Kit Harington) and Samwell Tarly (John Bradley) speak their Night's Watch vows before an ancient weirwood tree.* ✧ [OPPOSITE] *Jon Snow (Kit Harington) faces off against his fellow recruits in the Castle Black training yard.*

DESIGNING
THE WALL *AND* CASTLE BLACK

"I just want to stand on top of the Wall and piss off the edge of the world."
{ Tyrion Lannister }

DAVID BENIOFF *(executive producer, writer)*: The most important visual effects shot in the first episode is the Wall, which is fitting because the Wall might be the most crucial landmark in all of Westeros. It had to look both realistic and awe-inspiring, and the VFX team did an excellent job.

ADAM McINNES: Our aim with the Wall was to create a structure that was unquestionably built with ice but that also had some trademarks of the human engineering involved to construct it. The south side, where Castle Black resides, would be the business side of things. We'd see remnants of the tracks and outposts that would have been used to haul materials up and maintain it over the centuries. The north side had to be sheer, so that it was inconceivable that anyone or anything could ever scale the Wall, thus providing the perfect defense from the dark forces of the North. To build all of this we began with concept art and the physical construction of Castle Black in its location at Magheramorne quarry.

ROBBIE BOAKE *(locations coordinator)*: I remember first reading the season one breakdown and thinking, "Where am I going to find this?" Northern Ireland has many diverse locations, but not many seven-hundred-foot walls. So I was very pleased when I drove [production designer] Gemma Jackson over to Magheramorne, an old limestone quarry about twenty miles north of Belfast, and asked, "What do you think?" There it was! By complete coincidence, it ended up being the safest part of the quarry to build in.

ADAM McINNES: The justification for a more rocky base to the Wall was an engineering need to have solid material as a foundation to the ice, which obviously fits nicely with having a good high physical location to shoot within. The Special Effects team treated the surface of the rock to resemble ice and snow buildup. We then had the entire Castle Black and quarry-wall set scanned to provide the basis of an identical CG model, and extensive digital matte painting was used to finish the shots of the Wall seen in the show.

GEMMA JACKSON: It was Tom Martin, our amazing construction manager, who had the idea to use a real construction-site lift. So we bought one and the structure that went with it and dressed it ourselves. It was quite something, though I think it got stuck once or twice with actors inside!

DAVID BENIOFF: Gemma Jackson and her department outdid themselves with Castle Black. Of all the wonderful sets created for season one, it's probably my favorite. Directors loved shooting there because they could point the camera in any angle and never leave our world. There are no dead spots—when you stand in the middle of Castle Black, you really believe that you're *in* Castle Black.

GEMMA JACKSON (*production designer*): I started with the scripts and the descriptions found in George's book, but I also looked at a lot of material involving Eskimo cultures—or people living in igloos, which are

KIT HARINGTON (*Jon Snow*): **That set was pretty incredible. It was amazing to walk onto and almost identical to what I had in my head. I didn't realize it at the time, but working in the quarry, with the set built up against that huge wall, gave us actors a real sense of the importance of it. It would have been harder to have that sense of awe with just a green screen.**

filthy. They sleep on platforms all wrapped up in furs together. There are big tins of wax and grease, and there's blood from where they've killed seals. It's fascinating, very primal. I also became obsessed with Himalayan architecture. It often looks as if it's growing out of the rocks and the stones, and it has to withstand very strong

weather. Castle Black was a composite set featuring both exteriors and interiors, constructed up against a section of the quarry wall, and meant to represent the principal courtyard of a larger castle, the rest of which was built with CGI using concept art as a guide. All these castles along the Wall are falling apart, and Castle Black is one of

[above] *The Wall set.* ♦ [left] *Alliser Thorne (Owen Teale) in a "teachable moment" with Jon Snow (Kit Harington).* ♦ [opposite bottom left] *Early concept art, the Wall.* ♦ [opposite bottom right] *James Cosmo as Lord Commander Mormont*

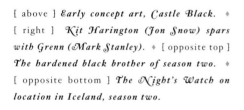

[above] *Early concept art, Castle Black.* ♦ [right] *Kit Harington (Jon Snow) spars with Grenn (Mark Stanley).* ♦ [opposite top] *The hardened black brother of season two.* ♦ [opposite bottom] *The Night's Watch on location in Iceland, season two.*

the few that even functions. It's a miserable place to be. So we decided to use timber and stone, raw materials to convey how grueling it would be to live there. It's a very monochromatic world of ice and wood and stone.

JOHN BRADLEY (*Samwell Tarly*): When I saw it for the first time, I thought, "Oh my God, this is huge! I need to up my game here. I need to be on the ball and perform as well as I can." But then I realized it was all

KIT HARINGTON: **I really loved shooting those fight scenes. Taking down three guys with a sword is a young actor's dream.**

there to *help* me perform as well as I could. So any worry I had about getting into the world of the show was completely dispelled then and there, simply because of how

impressive the set was and how immersed we became in it. It may be a TV set, but it's not the most pleasant place to be some days. Just to walk across that courtyard over those sharp stones, with the rain beating down and a heavy cloak on, there's no way your mind is going to be anywhere else. We'd shoot there all day, and the most comfortable place to rest was this big pile of rocks, so we'd all sit up there. That was comfort! We basically lived on that rock pile. ෧

COSTUMING
THE NIGHT'S WATCH

MICHELE CLAPTON (*costume designer*): These men wouldn't all wear the same color, the same shade of black. The Night's Watch is deteriorating, their numbers are dwindling, they have no money, so the clothes needed to reflect those circumstances. We worked with the idea that they've dyed their clothes black, which gives you different shades. And, of course, they have furs to keep warm, but everything always has to be drawn from what they can get nearby. It's all very dirty, very raw.

We also decided we'd keep the recruits in their own clothing, aside from crude standard-issue sparring armor. They don't don their

---

"Next time I see you, you'll be all in black."

{ Robb Stark }

"It was always my color."

{ Jon Snow }

---

black garb until they've passed muster and taken their Night's Watch vows. Many of the new recruits are plucked from prisons, so they don't have a cape or cloak. So within the recruits, there's a mixture of colors and fabrics, depending on where they came from. Sam, for instance, coming from a noble background, has a much higher standard of clothing.

Jon Snow's look initially came from Winterfell, but because he's the bastard, his clothes aren't quite of the same quality as his brothers and sisters. When he goes to the Wall, he keeps the same costume but introduces some new dark elements. Then of course, he goes fully black once he takes his vows. He retains his original black cape throughout the series; it's a piece of home, which makes sense for his character, I think. ❧

Jon Snow

"The next time we see each other,
we'll talk about your mother."

—Ned Stark to Jon Snow

The bastard son of Ned Stark, Jon was recognized by his father at birth and raised alongside his half brothers and half sisters at Winterfell, where he has always felt like an outsider. He grew up idolizing his father, yearning for the affection and approval Ned was never able to fully give. Jon seems to have found his place in the world with the Night's Watch, where he has become a natural leader and effective warrior when faced with the dangers beyond the Wall.

D. B. WEISS (*executive producer, writer*): Jon Snow is the closest this story has to a traditional hero, at least initially. But, as he does with all the major characters in this saga, George takes the familiar and turns it on, its head. Jon might be a hero, but his journey is anything but traditional.

DAVID BENIOFF: I feel like we saw every young actor in the UK, many of whom read several times for multiple roles, including Robb, Theon, Viserys, and Jon Snow. There were two audition pieces for Jon; one from the first episode and another from a scene late in the third novel, A *Storm of Swords*. Kit Harington stood out right from the start because he was able to fully embody Jon Snow at these two very different points in the story—the callow youth of the pilot and the seasoned warrior of future seasons.

KIT HARINGTON: I fell in love with him immediately because he's not a clichéd hero. He makes mistakes; he's possessed with a lot of self-loathing and doubt. He's lived his life as an outsider, since being born a bastard is a mark of shame in this world. While he's lucky to even be recognized by his father and raised alongside his brothers and sisters, he never truly feels part of the family, mainly because of the way he's treated by Catelyn, his stepmother.

MICHELLE FAIRLEY (*Catelyn Stark*): For Cat, he's a daily reminder of her Ned's infidelity, of his betrayal. I think she channels all the rage and hatred she felt toward Ned and inflicts it all on Jon. She can't mask it, and she can't suppress it. It's bigger than her.

KIT HARINGTON: There's that look I share with Catelyn in one of the first scenes of Episode 101, in the training yard. That sums up his whole childhood right there, what he's had to live with. I think, in some ways, everything he does, every relationship, comes back to the mother he never had, which gives him proper Freudian issues anytime he tries to get with a girl!

For Jon, the Night's Watch has always been, from quite an early age, something he knows he's going to do. He admires his uncle Benjen [played by Joseph Mawle], who's First Ranger in the Watch, and I think he senses that Benjen feels a bit of an outcast himself. He sees the Night's Watch as a noble calling, and the Wall as a place where he can become more than a bastard. Of course, he discovers the Wall and the Night's Watch to be very different from what he expected.

I think the first season is really about Jon losing his family: his father dead, his uncle missing beyond the Wall, his brothers and sisters separated, Robb leading a war. It has a huge impact on him, hardens him. He has to make the choice to leave his old life behind once and for all and dedicate himself to his new family, his Night's Watch brothers. The second season is about facing the dangers beyond the Wall and what it really means to be a black brother. He's tested in all kinds of unexpected ways.

[ABOVE LEFT] *Jon supervises archery practice with younger brother Bran in a scene from Episode 101.* ✤ [ABOVE] *The hardened black brother of season two.* ✤ [OPPOSITE] *John Bradley as Samwell Tarly.* ✤ [PREVIOUS PAGE] *Kit Harington as Jon Snow.*

"I always
wanted to be
a ranger."
—Jon Snow

"I always
wanted to be
a wizard."
—Samwell Tarly

SAMWELL TARLY

The firstborn son of a noble family, Sam was cast out by his disapproving father and forced to join the Night's Watch. Though Sam is a self-proclaimed coward who is initially bullied by his fellow recruits, his intelligence and quick thinking help him come into his own, and he eventually becomes Jon Snow's closest and most trusted friend.

JOHN BRADLEY: There was a moment in Episode 104, when we were doing the beating [in which timid Sam is abused by a fellow recruit] where I had a breakthrough moment. We'd done a few rehearsals, so I'd been beaten up a few times. [Director] Brian Kirk was lining up the shot, and I was lying there on the ground—no one was really paying any attention to me. I remember looking up at Kit, who was standing above me. Not speaking to anybody, almost to himself, he said, "Poor Sam." I was so pleased! I was assured in that moment about just how affecting this story line could be, seeing Kit the actor feeling something for the character in that moment. I knew we were on to something at that point.

KIT HARINGTON: At first glance, the dynamic between Jon and Sam might look like a "hero and his sidekick," but it's much more than that. Jon might start off as Sam's protector, but a real friendship develops almost immediately, and the two complement each other so well.

JOHN BRADLEY: My favorite scene from the first season is the "graduation" ceremony [in which the Night's Watch recruits are assigned their positions]. Sam can sense something's troubling Jon, and he uses his self-deprecation to bring a smile out of his friend. It showed a different side to Sam—how sharp he is in terms of emotional intelligence. Later on, there's the bit when Sam convinces Jon that being assigned to the stewards is a good thing, using rhetoric and logic to persuade him. It goes beyond friendship; Sam is actually becoming an influence on Jon.

KIT HARINGTON: John brings a lot of humor and intelligence to Sam. Like so many of these characters, just when you think you've got Sam figured out, he surprises you. He may appear to be a coward, but he's actually extraordinarily brave, one of the bravest characters in the series.

BEYOND the WALL

"We have other wars to fight. Out there."

—Lord Commander Mormont

DAVID BENIOFF: One of the challenges of the show is that we're traveling between wildly different environments and climates, often several times in an episode. Northern Ireland works wonderfully as a double for the Winterfell environs, the Riverlands, the Vale, and the Stormlands. But it's difficult to replicate the Land of Always Winter in Ireland: there are no major mountains; snowfall is sporadic and impossible to predict. Thankfully, Stuart Brisdon and the Special Effects team did a terrific job "snowing up" various locations for the first season.

In the second season, Jon Snow and the brothers of the Night's Watch venture far beyond the Wall in search of Benjen Stark and to learn why the wildlings have deserted their hamlets. Snowing up Craster's Keep—another masterful design by our ace in the hole, Gemma Jackson—worked well, but once Jon and company get to the Fist of the First Men and beyond, we weren't content with spraying bleached pulp on a muddy hilltop. We  felt we needed to shoot somewhere that looks as cold and glorious as the world we imagined while reading the books. So we shot the bulk of Jon Snow's season two story line in Iceland. It was immensely challenging, shooting in December, with about four and a half hours of shootable light per day, but the spectacular natural setting made it all worthwhile.

[TOP] *Early season two concept art, the Fist of the First Men.* ✣ [MIDDLE] *Jon Snow and Ygritte (played by Rose Leslie), a spirited wildling woman Jon encounters in the frozen wastelands beyond the Wall.* ✣ [OPPOSITE] *Craster's Keep.* ✣ [NEXT SPREAD] *Jon Snow outside Craster's Keep.*

Stark ⌡⌠

HOUSE STARK
A BRIEF HISTORY

"You were born in the long summer. You've never
known anything else.
But now winter is truly coming.
And in the winter, we must protect ourselves."
—Eddard "Ned" Stark

The leading house of the North, House Stark traces its descent from the First Men in the Age of Heroes. The family's founder, Brandon the Builder, was among those who established the Night's Watch in the aftermath of the Long Night. According to legend, Brandon enlisted the aid of giants and the powerful magic of the Children of the Forest to raise the Wall. He went on to build the ancestral seat of Winterfell and was crowned the first king in the North.

The Starks' reign lasted for thousands of years, even withstanding the invasion of the Andals. As the Children of the Forest were driven away and the southern kingdoms fell one by one, the North stood strong.

Eventually, Aegon Targaryen the Conqueror brought to an end the reign of the Kings of Winter. Aegon and his dragons destroyed the combined armies of the Reach and the Rock at the Field of Fire, and in order to spare the destruction of Winterfell and its people, King Torrhen Stark bent down and swore fealty to the Targaryen dynasty. Forever after, Torrhen Stark was known as "The King Who Knelt." The Starks continued to rule over their lands, but never again as kings, only as "wardens" of the North.

The Starks are an ancient and proud family, mindful of their rich history and traditions and fiercely devoted to one another. Much like their sigil, the direwolf, their ancestors are the stuff of legend in the North. And their family words, "Winter Is Coming," serve as a reminder of their beginnings in the wake of the Long Night and a warning of things to come.

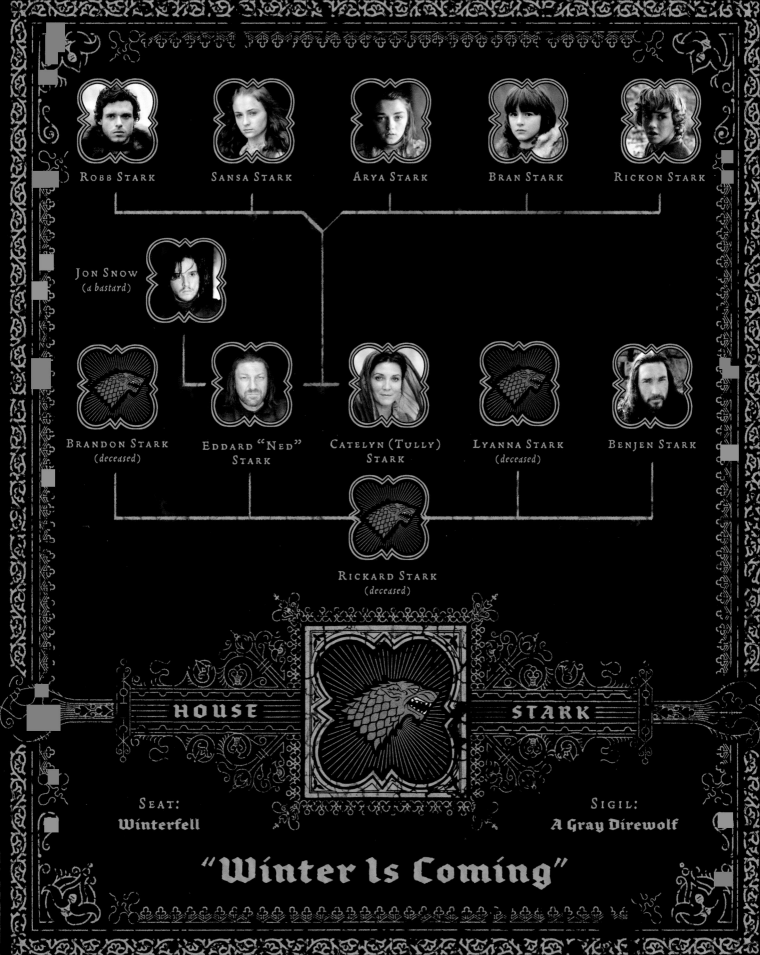

ROBB STARK   SANSA STARK   ARYA STARK   BRAN STARK   RICKON STARK

JON SNOW
(a bastard)

BRANDON STARK
(deceased)

EDDARD "NED"
STARK

CATELYN (TULLY)
STARK

LYANNA STARK
(deceased)

BENJEN STARK

RICKARD STARK
(deceased)

HOUSE STARK

SEAT:
Winterfell

SIGIL:
A Gray Direwolf

"Winter Is Coming"

CREATING WINTERFELL

D. B. WEISS (*executive producer, writer*): The show pretty much begins in Winterfell, and the Starks were very much the anchor of the first season, so designing their home was no small task. It was difficult because it needed to feel like the kind of place the Starks would come from: solid, trustworthy, simple, grounded, and . . . well, stark. But it also needed to be unique and not just pulled into the orbit of "standard twelfth-century Scottish castle." We shot pieces of the pilot at Doune Castle, a medieval stronghold in central Scotland—which is an amazing place, not to mention the location for much of *Monty Python and the Holy Grail*—but we wanted to introduce different elements and influences to keep Winterfell looking like a real place yet unlike any real place we'd ever been.

"There must always be a Stark in Winterfell."

{ Catelyn Stark }

GEMMA JACKSON (*production designer*): Doune set the tone, but Winterfell has really evolved from season one to season two. As it wasn't practical to return to Scotland for the filming of the series, an exact replica of Doune's great hall was built on the soundstage in Belfast, along with other Winterfell interior sets.

ROBBIE BOAKE (*locations coordinator*): For Winterfell's courtyard and outer walls,

we were fortunate to find Castle Ward, an eighteenth-century property owned by the National Trust. We were able to nestle the central Winterfell courtyard within an existing set of buildings, and the S-shaped approach to the main Winterfell entrance represented a great opportunity to bring King Robert's procession [in Episode 101] through the outer workings of Winterfell and into the heart of the castle. For season two, the story dictated that the Winterfell set be expanded, so it was rebuilt from the ground up at the Moneyglass Estate, near the village of Toome.

GEMMA JACKSON: In some ways, Winterfell is probably the most medieval of the worlds we visit. But we wanted the exterior

ISAAC HEMPSTEAD-WRIGHT *(Bran Stark)*: I think the raven is sort of a symbol of things to come for Bran—these sort of ancient powers that he's slowly learning how to use. And he's not sure about them; he's actually kind of scared of them. I think there will come a point where he has to use them for some kind of purpose. Or maybe he'll just go insane because of them, I don't know!

[above and opposite] *Concept art, Winterfell.* ♦ [left] *Concept art, a bird's-eye view of Winterfell's courtyard.* ♦ [below] *Concept art, "The Three-Eyed Raven."* ♦ [next spread] *Osha (Natalia Tena) with Maester Luwin (Donald Sumpter) in his final moments in the shadow of Winterfell's weirwood.*

to have another essence to it, and it went through a lot of iterations. In the end, I think we came up with something quite original looking, a real hybrid.

D. B. WEISS: Gemma's inspiration was to cross-pollinate several different types of English and Scottish castle designs with elements of Scandinavian wooden architecture, drawn largely from the magnificent stave churches in Norway and Sweden.

GEMMA JACKSON: For Winterfell's godswood, the first step was to find the perfect tree to serve as its weirwood. That was difficult. There are a lot of beech trees in Northern Ireland, and I was trying to find something else, something more gnarly—but, in the end, we found this particular beech that worked at a separate location. The godswood set was designed and dressed around it.

ADAM McINNES (*VFX supervisor, season one*): The tree was selected for its unusual shape and was painted white on top of a coat of latex to preserve the tree. Finished, it was ready to shoot up to a height of about fifteen feet. This meant most shots could be accomplished in-camera with only wide shots requiring visual effects to top it up.

GEMMA JACKSON: That tree worked so well it was re-dressed and used to represent a different weirwood north of the Wall, where Jon Snow takes his Night's Watch vows [in Episode 107]. I found the godswood set magical. We inked the water in the pools so it had that black reflective quality. It was very still, almost like a sanctuary for Ned and his family. There is a place near where I lived as a child called "The Silent Pool." As the story goes, a village couple jumped into it together and perished, and ever since there hasn't been a sound. It's beautiful there, and that inspired me. I always try to draw on things that have personally affected me over the years. ❧

COSTUMING WINTERFELL

MICHELE CLAPTON (costume designer): I used medieval Northern Europe as a starting point, but the skirts in the men's costumes have a Japanese look to them. We were never bound by the rules of any particular time period.

First, you have to think about what they need, the practicality of it, what materials they have readily available. We also decided we'd have no jewelry, so there's a lot of embroidery and embellishment in the women's clothing, as well as these lovely padded neck pieces. As for the men, most of the armor is leather with some metal inside, but rarely close to the skin due to the cold. The fur collars were meant to be wolf pelts for the adults, the children have rabbit, and the peasants have collars stuffed with sheep's wool.

We have a lot of blues and grays, murkier colors that seemed right for the harsh northern climates. The Starks represent a

[above] *Costume concept art for Ned, Catelyn, and Sansa.* ♦ [opposite top and left] *Ned and Catelyn in northern furs.* ♦ [opposite right] *Sansa's costume made real.*

───※───

warm family unit, so the blues of their costumes are rather warm. But within the family, the various personalities are reflected in what they wear. For example, Sansa is in a slightly cooler blue. And the design of the nobles' clothes spirals outward; what they wear inspires the people around them, from the ladies-in-waiting to the household staff, on down to the peasants.

It's important that the costumes reflect each character's individual journey. I always like to tell a story through the clothes, and I think it helps the actors, too. Sansa is a perfect example of this. She leaves Winterfell

for a life at court early in the first season and begins to take on more and more of Queen Cersei's traits as season one goes on. By the end of the season, she's really starting to look like her. But in season two, her dresses are destroyed in the first half of the season, and Sansa starts reverting back to her childhood. The colors start coming down, and she's trying to alter things back to where she was. So at the end of it, she's wearing something closer to her mother's look. She's come full circle.

By contrast, Ned was never seen adopting any of the clothing styles in King's Landing. He had four different looks, a couple of which were slightly smarter, but Ned generally chose to keep things functional and practical. To that end, he'd often be seen in the padded linen skirts with the leather doublet, sometimes with a cape. Later in the season, as he began to sense trouble brewing, he started wearing his leather armor. 🦢

EDDARD "NED" STARK

> "I'm a northman.
> I belong here with you, not
> down south in that rat's nest
> they call a capital."
>
> —Ned Stark

The patriarch of House Stark, Warden of the North, and Lord of Winterfell, Ned Stark is a northerner through and through. He is disciplined, strong, and possessed of a powerful sense of honor and justice. But beneath his hard exterior, he is a loving husband and father. He is steadfast in his loyalty to King Robert, his best friend since childhood, whose throne he helped secure. Haunted and weary from years of waging war, he is compelled to leave his beloved home and family to serve Robert in his court at King's Landing—a decision with fatal consequences.

[LEFT] Eddard Stark (Sean Bean) in the solitude of Winterfell's godswood.

SEAN BEAN (*Ned Stark*): The Starks are only seen as a whole family for just a short time before they're split apart. They're dignified and noble, but also down-to-earth, honest people. Ned loves his wife. He loves his kids. And for him to have to leave his home not knowing if he'll see them again, it's tragic really. All Ned wants to do is live his life in Winterfell with his family.

FRANK DOELGER (*producer*): I think a key component of the success of both George's book and David and Dan's adaptation is that Ned is a great way in for the audience. When Robert comes to Winterfell and says, "Come to King's Landing," everything revolves around that. While there are all these big, colorful characters bouncing all over the place, you have solid Ned in the center, trying to do the right thing.

D. B. WEISS: There were only two actors we knew we absolutely needed to make the show work the way we envisioned it. Sean Bean was one of them. It's a good thing he liked the script. He's a consummate professional, able to say so much without saying anything, and so utterly in control of what he's doing. There would be times when you'd think, "Hmmm, he doesn't seem to be doing much. . . ." And then you'd see the performance cut together, and it would just leave you speechless.

Sean also belongs to a rare, dying breed: the believable, manly tough guy. Ned is a good man, upright and honorable to a fault, but he's also a man of violence. Sean can make you believe he's a man who's made his place in the world by killing other men. There was a time when lots of recognizable actors had this quality—John Wayne, Clint Eastwood, Kirk Douglas, Charlton Heston. Now, not so much. Sean has this quality, and a related but not identical one: he can occupy this kind of period successfully.

As if that weren't enough, he's a joy to work with. It was truly an honor and a pleasure to have him, even if he did almost get several of us killed in a pub in rural Scotland by being a little too vocal about rooting for the Celtics football team instead of the Rangers. Okay, maybe a lot too vocal. Apparently, this is not advised in certain parts of rural Scotland.

MICHELLE FAIRLEY (*Catelyn Stark*): Sean was absolutely fantastic. He exemplified Ned, that quiet strength. He may not be much of a talker, but he can do a lot with a look. And you felt safe with him, trusted him, which is key for those intense, emotional scenes.

KIT HARINGTON (*Jon Snow*): It was thrilling and hugely intimidating shooting my handful of scenes with Sean. Jon's tricky relationship with his father is very much the core of who he is, and I think it was vital to establish the kind of complicated love they have for each other. That final scene of ours, when we say good-bye on the Kingsroad, was extremely powerful. I think Sean does some of the best work of his career in that scene, when he starts to talk about Jon's mother.

MAISIE WILLIAMS (*Arya Stark*): We'd done the pilot together, but I didn't have that many scenes with Sean. When we got to the series, the first big scenes I shot were with him. It was scary at first because here's this man I've grown up seeing on the telly, but Sean was great to work with. I actually think it helped doing those scenes first because it gave me a lot of confidence moving forward.

ALAN TAYLOR (*director*): He was the heart of the first season, the moral center—whether he was on-screen or not. Sean was perfect in the role because he carries so much soulfulness with him.

SEAN BEAN: Ned's decent. He's strong. He's sympathetic. I think he grounds the story and gives a sense of direction. I just love the character.

[ABOVE AND OPPOSITE] *Sean Bean as Ned Stark.*

"At times I feel like I'm being torn apart. If only there were five of me, one for each child."

—Catelyn Stark

CATELYN STARK

Catelyn, the wife to Ned Stark and mother of his five trueborn children, is not a native northerner, having grown up far south in the Riverlands. Catelyn was originally betrothed to Ned's older brother, but when he was killed, she fulfilled her duty by marrying Ned and securing the alliance between their two houses. She came to love Ned deeply, and her perceptiveness and honesty have made her his most trusted counselor.

DAVID BENIOFF (*executive producer, writer*): I first saw Michelle Fairley when she played Emilia in the Donmar Warehouse's production of *Othello* in London. Emilia's not a character I generally notice in *Othello*. Iago's wife? Who cares? But Michelle was so absurdly good that I left the theater thinking, "Who the hell was that? And is she available?"

D. B. WEISS: Catelyn is a tricky role. In the first episode, someone could be excused for thinking she was going to fade into a more subordinate "dutiful wife and mother" role. But from the second episode onward, a very different person comes to the fore: a woman who loathes the sight of Jon Snow as a walking reminder of her husband's infidelity, and most of all, a woman willing to do anything and everything to defend her family, to the point of recklessness and beyond. Michelle has a rare ability to play all the facets of this character: the warmth and love, but also the determination, the steel, the rage. Sometimes she plays them all in the same scene. She has a gift for generating family chemistry—her love for Ned and her children feels very real. Chemistry is an intangible thing, but when it's missing, you definitely feel it.

MICHELLE FAIRLEY: She's extremely strong and incredibly loyal. The words of Cat's house, House Tully, are "Family, Duty, Honor," and that's how she's tried to live her life. When she was a girl, she was engaged to Ned's elder brother, but when he was killed in the war, she was unwavering in her duty and married Ned in his place. What I find lovely

about her is that she grew to love him and forge a real bond with him. When they part for what turns about to be the last time [in Episode 103], it's a huge loss.

BRIAN KIRK (*director, season one*): The Ned/Catelyn relationship was very satisfying to develop because of the qualities Sean and Michelle brought to the roles. They were fiercely individual, but they had an intense romantic chemistry. Each was a natural leader. Both were tough but sensitive—strong individuals who appreciated working as a team. They were required to be parents and warriors, and this dichotomy perfectly captured the conflict between love and duty that was at the heart of the story.

RICHARD MADDEN (*Robb Stark*): I share the majority of my scenes with Michelle, especially in the second season, and she's a tremendous actress. We've grown very close working on these intense, emotional scenes. I think Catelyn and Robb have the closest, and maybe the most open and honest, relationship in the Stark family. Circumstances have really thrust them together, and certainly the loss of Ned has. They're realizing how much they really need each other, even though they're often at loggerheads.

MICHELLE FAIRLEY: At her core, she's a mother. This is a huge part of her story, especially in season two, after Ned has been killed. Her children are everything to her, and she'll stop at nothing to protect them.

ROBB STARK

"There sits the only king
I mean to bend my knee to!
The King in the North!"

—"Greatjon" Umber

The eldest of the Stark children, Robb is a brave young man and a skilled fighter who is committed to defending his family and upholding his father's code of ethics. He is tested as never before when his father leaves for King's Landing and he must assume the duties of Lord of Winterfell. After Ned's tragic death, Robb calls his banners and rallies the North to war against the Lannisters, whereupon he is crowned the "King in the North"—the first in three centuries.

D. B. WEISS: At first we just liked Richard because he was the odds-on favorite for 2009's Best-Dressed Man in Scotland Award. He did indeed win—and in addition to his clothes, we got an amazing talent. He manages to be both period-appropriate and totally natural. When you're standing in front of an army of armored men making grand post-battle speeches, hokeyness and stiltedness are definite dangers, but Richard is incapable of these things. There's an easygoing quality to the character that comes from Richard himself, and it acts like armor against all ponderousness.

RICHARD MADDEN: Robb is one of the few Starks that isn't a POV character in the books, which gave me a lot of freedom in building the character. I based a lot of him on Ned, as he has so much respect and admiration for his father. I think that's the core of his character at the start of the series. But you begin to discover that Robb possesses some of the emotional volatility of Catelyn as well. What's interesting about Robb is he's someone trying to play an adult male, when he's not

really there yet. I don't think he really wants to be the King in the North. I think he just wants peace. As the second season goes on, he keeps winning these battles, but the real victory seems so far away.

[ABOVE] Robb and his brothers Jon Snow & Bran, in the series' first episode. ❖ [OPPOSITE] Richard Madden as Robb Stark.

Sansa, Arya, and Bran

SANSA: The eldest daughter of Ned Stark, Sansa is lovely, graceful, demure—the perfect, proper young lady. At the start of the story, she is a firm believer in romance, chivalry, and tradition. She learns the hard truth about such fantasies with the death of her father and the constant abuse from her fiancé, Joffrey Baratheon, transforming her from dreamer to survivor. ⊠ **ARYA:** The youngest daughter of Ned Stark, Arya is a tomboy who'd much rather be riding, sparring, and playing at swords with her brothers. Arya is whip-smart, athletic, and defiant of authority. She accompanies her father on his journey to King's Landing, along with her older sister, Sansa, with whom she does not get along. In King's Landing, she begins to train in the ways of swordplay, skills that come in handy when tragedy strikes her family and she's forced to survive on her own. ⊠ **BRAN:** Growing up, Bran was a rambunctious boy, whose favorite hobby was climbing up and down the towers of Winterfell. His dreams of one day serving as a knight of the Kingsguard were shattered when he was pushed from a tower and paralyzed. Soon after his fall, he began having intense and prophetic dreams.

GEORGE R. R. MARTIN (*executive producer, author*): The kids are a huge part of the story, in many ways the central part of the story. And I always intended to separate them and set them on own their own paths.

D. B. WEISS: W. C. Fields said, "Never work with animals or children." He was almost right. Casting the Stark children was easily the most terrifying part of the entire casting process. There have been a few movies, but I can't think of another TV show, where the weight of so much adult material rests on the shoulders of people under the age of fifteen. And not just one of them, three of them.

GEORGE R. R. MARTIN: There are a lot of kid actors out there, but they don't usually have to do any serious acting. Our show is different in that the kids have to carry the drama for a huge percentage of the story. They're central to everything that's going on.

D. B. WEISS: The odds of them all being strong actors were slim. The odds of them all being strong actors and none of them being entitled demons raised by slavering nightmare show-parents were about zero. But through the miraculous digging of casting directors Nina Gold and Robert Sterne, we found Sophie, Maisie, and Isaac. Each of them exceeded expectations to a tremendous degree. In very specific ways, each has such a powerful screen presence, such an amazing gift. Their work ethic keeps us honest, their enthusiasm reminds us why we're doing this in the first place . . . and their parents are all lovely and decent people. With their poise, professionalism, and talent, these three reach back across the decades and give W. C. Fields the finger.

[NEAR LEFT] *Sophie Turner as Sansa Stark.* ✣ [TOP LEFT] *Maisie Williams as Arya Stark.* ✣ [BOTTOM LEFT] *Isaac Hempstead-Wright as Bran Stark.*

ISAAC HEMPSTEAD-WRIGHT: Kristian Nairn (Hodor) is such a lovely guy—really funny on set, and I'm always singing songs to him. I miss him a lot when I'm off set, at home. It's a good thing we get along, since he has to carry me around so much.

[above] *Sporting a Stark guard helmet, Arya watches King Robert's arrival.* ◆ [below] *Sansa Stark and her direwolf, Lady.* ◆ [opposite] *After losing the use of his legs, Bran's primary mode of transport is Hodor (Kristian Nairn), a Winterfell servant with giant's blood.*

SOPHIE TURNER (*Sansa Stark*): I think I'm getting to know Sansa better. As I age, Sansa ages, so I like to relate my development from a child to a young adult to Sansa growing up as well. I can understand the changes that she goes through because I am living them at the same time as she is. I am constantly discovering new things about her.

MAISIE WILLIAMS: When I first heard about Arya, I figured, "Oh, she's a tomboy, and she doesn't do what she's told." But after playing her for nearly two years, I've learned a lot more about her. Everything in her world is black and white. She finds it weird how people can say "maybe." With her, it's either "yes" or "no." You can't have anything in between! But I think she's a bit misunderstood. People think she's disobedient, but there's more to it. She just wants an actual answer. She doesn't want people to faff around. She's a lot like her father that way.

[BELOW] *Arya spars with her "dancing master" Syrio Forel (Miltos Yerolemou) as proud father Ned looks on.* ❖
[OPPOSITE] *Arya in season two.*

ISAAC HEMPSTEAD-WRIGHT: Bran and I have sort of grown up together. We're the same age, more or less, though he has a few more challenges than I do!

SOPHIE TURNER: I do believe Sansa possesses an inner strength that not many of the other characters have. She appears fragile on the outside, but as the show goes on, you realize that she is not as tender as people think. She sometimes gets negative feedback from the fans, and I think it is because she has been such a predictably naive teenage girl that people often get annoyed at her. In season two, there's a stronger side to Sansa, and hopefully viewers will warm to her more. Sansa of season one was a spoiled, naive, innocent young girl who strongly believed in fairy tales and true love. Sansa of season two is so different. She is strong, independent, and fairly manipulative. This season Sansa only thinks about survival. That is her main priority, just to survive, and most of her innocence and hope is gone. She becomes much more clever.

MAISIE WILLIAMS: I like Arya—she's always up to something. There's never a dull moment. She's always got a weapon in hand or is climbing up a statue or hitting someone with a stick. You don't expect a child to have this sort of role. And she has killer lines, which is a bonus. I think people like Arya because she stands up for herself and others and says what's on her mind.

ISAAC HEMPSTEAD-WRIGHT: Bran's disability is the most interesting thing for me. He's had to undergo such a dramatic transformation, from happy-go-lucky, carefree kid to someone who has to depend on others for everything. He's trying to deal with it, but I think there's a dark side underneath. Another big part of his story is how he deals with losing his family: his father dying; his mother, sisters, and older brothers going away. He has to grow up really fast and take on a lot of responsibility.

MAISIE WILLIAMS: I found a picture on the Internet of all the Stark children in the first episode. There's Arya flicking the pigeon pie, and Sansa looking up at Joffrey all happy, and we're all in our little Winterfell outfits. Then, underneath, it shows all of us in the last episode of season one: me with short hair, Sansa staring up at the heads. It was a really powerful picture. All that happened in ten episodes! It made me think Arya didn't really know what she had until it was gone.

MAISIE WILLIAMS: I found the sword fighting difficult because of the left-handed business. I'd just got the part, and I remember my mum was out in the garden reading the book. She says, 'By the way, Arya's left-handed.' And I said, 'Oh, that's going to be hard' [Maisie is right-handed]. And she said, 'Well, I don't think they'll make you do it left-handed.' And I said, 'But it'd be cool if I did.' We heard about all the people on the Internet wanting the show to be like the books, so I thought I would try it and see how it goes. Learning the routines was a lot like learning a piece of choreography, it's just that you have a sword in your hand.

III King's La

nding [House Lannister
House Baratheon]

KING'S LANDING
A BRIEF HISTORY

 *Three centuries ago, Aegon Targaryen, his sister-wives, and their army sailed from Dragonstone and landed on the eastern coast of Westeros. On this spot, where a handful of simple fisherfolk dwelled, Aegon began his conquest of the Seven Kingdoms, building his first crude holdfast on the highest hill out of wood and earth. The holdfast would one day become the Red Keep, and the site where Aegon first came ashore would become his capitol: King's Landing.*

With a burgeoning and diverse population of some half million people, King's Landing is the largest and fastest-growing city in the realm. Sprawling over three hills and along the shore of Blackwater Bay, its manses, storehouses, brothels, and markets pile on top of one another and are surrounded by a high city wall with seven gates. Its busy harbor is the center of the world's trade and a gateway to the great continent of Essos, across the Narrow Sea.

The city is dominated by the Red Keep, an enormous castle atop Aegon's High Hill, overlooking Blackwater Bay. Construction of the keep began under Aegon but was not completed until the reign of his son, Maegor. Known as Maegor the Cruel, he oversaw the construction of a labyrinthine network of tunnels and secret passageways, which runs throughout the keep and underneath the city. Once the keep was completed, Maegor earned his nickname by executing every architect, stonemason, and builder, so he might be the only man with knowledge of its many secrets. This monument to the power of the monarchy proudly flew the three-headed dragon banner of House Targaryen from its battlements until Robert Baratheon rebelled and took the Iron Throne for himself.

King's Landing is celebrated far and wide as the center of politics and culture in the known world, but it is also a dangerous place, its hot climate breeding many a plot and intrigue. It is here where the Game of Thrones is truly played.

[BELOW] *The Red Keep and King's Landing.*
[OPPOSITE] *The king's Small Council.*

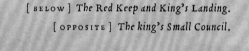

CREATING KING'S LANDING

D. B. WEISS *(executive producer, writer)*: We knew from the outset that King's Landing and the Red Keep were arguably going to be the most important of our worlds, for the simple reason that so much of the story ends up taking place there. The mandate here was to create a place that makes people feel the way the Starks feel when they first arrive at King's Landing in the third episode. The Red Keep needed to be a structure that dwarfed the architecture of Winterfell, a building whose size and design bespeak elegance, danger, callousness, and intrigue.

To do this meant bending reality a bit. The show's viewers live in the modern world, and when people are used to hundred-story buildings, even the largest piece of real medieval architecture isn't going to have the effect on them that we were going for. So we had to walk the line between what was strictly realistic historically speaking and the free-for-all that characterizes a lot of the design work in the genre. The art department and the VFX team have done a fabulous job so far—the second season's Throne Room design is an especially high point for me, a

perfect embodiment of Joffrey Baratheon's personality in iron and stone.

Since the structure and city were much larger than anything we could ever hope to build, visual effects in the form of digital matte paintings and set extensions were a part of the conception from the beginning. If we are lucky enough for the show to continue, King's Landing and the Red Keep will grow and evolve with it.

FRANK DOELGER *(producer)*: We shot the majority of the King's Landing exteriors for season one in Malta, which worked very well for our needs at the time. But we felt we'd exhausted what it had to offer. Starting with season two, we're filming in Dubrovnik, Croatia. It's a city that grew up over centuries and has many features similar to King's Landing: it's fortified, surrounded by enormous walls, and guards over an important waterway. And the views from the walls and fortifications are fantastic.

[opposite top] *Jon Arryn, former Hand of the King, lies in state before the Iron Throne.* ♦ [opposite bottom] *The crowned stag of Baratheon is prominently displayed in the king's royal box at the tourney grounds.* ♦ [above and left] *Various Red Keep interiors, including the chamber of the Hand.*

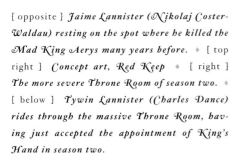

[opposite] *Jaime Lannister (Nikolaj Coster-Waldau) resting on the spot where he killed the Mad King Aerys many years before.* ♦ [top right] *Concept art, Red Keep* ♦ [right] *The more severe Throne Room of season two.* ♦ [below] *Tywin Lannister (Charles Dance) rides through the massive Throne Room, having just accepted the appointment of King's Hand in season two.*

GEMMA JACKSON (*production designer*): King's Landing is very much a character in the story, and George R. R. Martin has a very detailed layout in the books. But obviously, it's impossible to build all of it. The city itself is a combination of a lot of locations: Malta in season one, Dubrovnik in season two, as well as a few sets and locations in Northern Ireland. We've also utilized Malta and Croatia for the courtyards, gardens, and battlements of the Red Keep.

There are two principal interior sets for the Red Keep. The first is a composite set with several rooms and corridors, including the chamber of the Hand. It's a large set, but it's still only four rooms, which are meant to represent all the chambers in the Red Keep! For example, the Small Hall of the Tower of the Hand is frequently re-dressed and used as Cersei's bedchamber and Robert's bedchamber, among others.

The other major set is the enormous Throne Room, which has gone through huge changes from season one to season two. At first, it had a rather decorative look with leaves on the pillars, but in season two, Joffrey came in with this testosterone-filled madness and gave it a makeover. So the leaves went away. The pillars now have these huge braziers on them, which when lit up give the room a rather terrifying look, even transforming the hunting frieze on the wall from something pastoral into something sinister. I love how the set reflects the changes in the story, as the second season is much darker than the first. ❧

The
IRON THRONE

 he Iron Throne is the
seat of power in the
Seven Kingdoms. Aegon
the Conqueror ordered
this revered (and cov-
eted) throne to be made up of the swords of
his vanquished enemies. Aegon's dragon,
Balerion the Black Dread, melted down
the swords and sealed them in dragonflame.

GEMMA JACKSON (*production designer*): I'm so
pleased with how the Iron Throne turned out. We wanted
to make something totally unique but also realistic—as
realistic as a throne of swords sealed in dragonfire can
look. Gavin Jones, our supervising prop maker, executed
it brilliantly. You can see why so many characters want it
for themselves.

JACK GLEESON (*Joffrey Baratheon*): In between takes,
when we're waiting around, I'll just stay seated in the Iron
Throne—I don't get off! It does have this power. Luckily, the
designers made it more comfortable for the actor than it's supposed to be in the story. Seated up there, looking down on
everyone, it's hard not to tap into that power-mad, superiority
complex that Joff has.

[OPPOSITE] *The Iron Throne in its chilling finality.* ❖ [TOP] *Joffrey on the throne in*
season two. ❖ [BOTTOM] *Early Iron Throne concept art.*

COSTUMING KING'S LANDING

MICHELE CLAPTON (*costume designer*): One of the mandates early on was to make King's Landing very distinct from the traditional medieval courts and cities one usually finds in these types of stories. It's warm and sunny; the climate is somewhat Mediterranean. It was a lot of fun to do because King's Landing is a port city, so we have access to color, silks, much more variety. And the Lannisters are a huge presence, so there's a lot of red, but also pale greens and saffron yellows, and you can use jewelry. There are a lot of choices.

As with Winterfell and other regions, I started with the most prominent characters because, in theory, the people are influenced by the head of the society. So Cersei has these kimono-style, wraparound dresses that influence the other ladies at court and in the city. Even the prostitutes in Littlefinger's brothel wear a similar-style dress, albeit in a different way. Then there's Jaime, with his asymmetrical coat, whose influence trickles down to the male characters.

ARMOR:

SIMON BRINDLE (*costume armor supervisor*): I loved the opportunity to work on this series, as you're not tied down to any one period. This was so freeing. I was intrigued by Michele's initial designs for the Kingsguard and the Lannister guard. She was looking at eastern influences, Asian, Indian—unusual references for this sort of thing—which she mixed with recognizable touchstones from western medieval European armor.

MICHELE CLAPTON: This was a challenge, as I've never designed armor before. We started with the Kingsguard, which are totally white in the books. But we felt that wouldn't translate well on-screen, so we worked gold into the design, while keeping the signature white cloak. ❧

SIMON BRINDLE: The Lannister armor is more militaristic, intimidating, sinister—with a Japanese influence that's quite disarming. With the Gold Cloaks, there's a Persian influence in keeping with the Mediterranean look of the city.

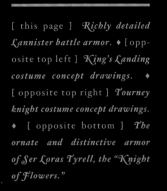

HOUSE LANNISTER

A BRIEF HISTORY

"And so he spoke, and so he spoke, That lord of Castamere,
But now the rains weep o'er his hall, With no one there to hear."

—from "The Rains of Castamere"

The wealthiest and most influential of the noble houses, the Lannisters of Casterly Rock lord over the gold-rich Westerlands. They descend from the Andal invaders and, through the female bloodline, from Lann the Clever—a legendary trickster from the Age of Heroes who swindled the Rock from its original occupant: House Casterly. The Lannisters reigned as kings of the Rock for thousands of years until the coming of Aegon the Conqueror.

The last of the Lannister kings, King Loren initially refused to bend the knee to Aegon. Joining forces with Mern of the Reach, he met the Targaryen host in open battle. Aegon unleashed all three of his dragons, slaughtering four thousand men at what came to be known as the Field of Fire. King Mern perished in dragonflame, and Loren wisely surrendered. He went on to aid the Targaryens in their further conquest of Westeros. As a reward for their service, the Lannisters were appointed Lords Paramount of the Westerlands and Wardens of the West.

The lion of Lannister prospered over the centuries, but it was nearly brought to ruin when Tytos Lannister, a weak and ineffectual man, lorded over Casterly Rock. Tytos was openly mocked at court, even by his own bannermen, and brought the family to the brink of ruin with a string of poor investments. When House Reyne of Castamere, a sworn vassal of the Lannisters, dared to rise up against Tytos, it was his eldest son, Tywin, who crushed the rebellion. Tywin led his troops in a merciless assault of Castamere and eradicated House Reyne. His victory was immortalized in the ballad "The Rains of Castamere," which has become an anthem of House Lannister.

In the years that followed, Tywin's military brilliance, political savvy, and shrewd business mind restored the name of Lannister to its proper glory. Lord Tywin served as an uncommonly powerful Hand of the King to Aerys the Second for twenty years, but he resigned in protest after a falling out with the king, who was steadily descending into madness. When Robert Baratheon rebelled against Aerys, House Lannister remained neutral, but pledged its support to Robert's side after his victory on the Trident. To secure the capital city for Robert, Tywin Lannister commanded the sacking of King's Landing. Then, upon taking the Iron Throne, King Robert made Tywin's daughter, Cersei, his queen.

The official words for the lion of Lannister are "Hear Me Roar!" but a more appropriate (and foreboding) motto is more commonly used: "A Lannister Always Pays His Debts."

GEORGE R. R. MARTIN: In the books, part of my intent with the Lannisters is to see them first from the outside. They seem villainous, but then when you're in their head, and the story is told from their point of view, you get a new perspective. Maybe they still seem villainous, but you begin to understand them a little more and why they do what they do. And also, hopefully, all these characters are changing.

CHARLES DANCE (*Tywin Lannister*): To be a Lannister is to be proud of the Lannister lineage and their place in society. Tywin believes that his right to rule his bit of the Seven Kingdoms is, like that of so many rulers, divine.

LENA HEADEY (*Cersei Lannister*): The Starks are "honorable" and "admirable." The Lannisters are survivors. If they have to play a sneaky hand, they do, and they don't see anything wrong with that.

PETER DINKLAGE (*Tyrion Lannister*): The Lannisters are all very good at what they do, but it seems that all the cards were dealt to the wrong people. Cersei wants the power but is a woman in a male-dominated world. Jaime is the golden child who wants to avoid all things politic. Tyrion is the brilliant politician who isn't taken seriously. Cersei and Tyrion have a lot in common, which is why their relationship is so damaged. They see each other very clearly for who they really are. Being born into such wealth and privilege has afforded them all great opportunities—Tyrion, as he has said, "may have been left in the woods to die" if born under different circumstances—but it has clearly affected them at the family dinner table.

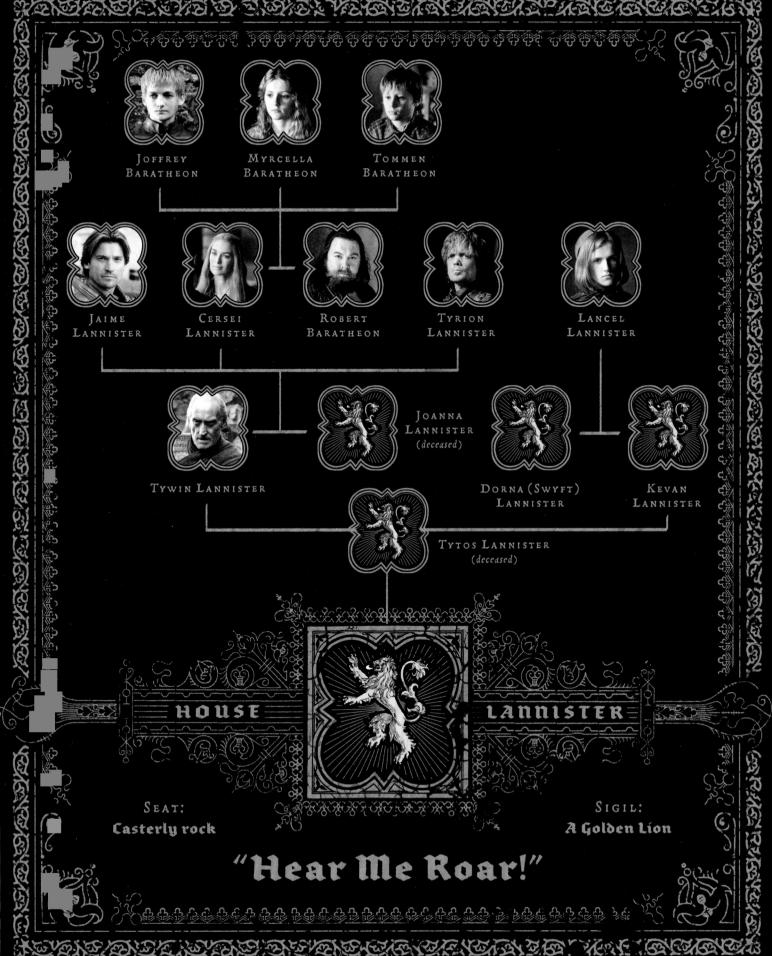

JOFFREY
BARATHEON

MYRCELLA
BARATHEON

TOMMEN
BARATHEON

JAIME
LANNISTER

CERSEI
LANNISTER

ROBERT
BARATHEON

TYRION
LANNISTER

LANCEL
LANNISTER

TYWIN LANNISTER

JOANNA
LANNISTER
(deceased)

DORNA (SWYFT)
LANNISTER

KEVAN
LANNISTER

TYTOS LANNISTER
(deceased)

HOUSE LANNISTER

SEAT:
Casterly rock

SIGIL:
A Golden Lion

"Hear Me Roar!"

Tywin Lannister

"The lion doesn't concern himself with the opinions of the sheep."
—Tywin Lannister

The powerful and wealthy patriarch of House Lannister, Tywin is Lord of Casterly Rock and Warden of the West and holds a great deal of influence at court and throughout Westeros. He harbors a deep hatred for his youngest son, Tyrion, partly because Tyrion is a dwarf but also because Tywin's beloved wife died giving birth to him. Even so, when Tyrion is taken captive by Catelyn Stark, the family's honor is at stake and Tywin takes up arms against the Starks and their allies in retaliation.

DAVID BENIOFF (*executive producer, writer*): As soon as Dan and I sold the pitch to HBO, we started playing that game of "Who should play so-and-so in the series?" Years and years slipped away before we actually cast the show, but we constantly talked about which actors we'd love to see in which role. Tywin Lannister is a particularly tricky part to play. Dan told me to watch the BBC production of *Bleak House*, and in particular Charles Dance, the actor playing Tulkinghorn. So I did. After that, there was never any doubt. We never auditioned another actor, and we never seriously considered anyone else.

CHARLES DANCE: Tywin, whilst being seen to be coldly cruel and domineering, shows, as the story progresses, occasional "chinks in his armor." He's an enigma, and enigmatic characters are always attractive—to me, anyway! I'm not sure that I would label Tywin a villain—certainly not compared with some of the villains I've played. However, if he is, then unless the character is obviously insane, I look for the justification of his villainy.

DANIEL MINAHAN (*director, season one*): I love that I got to introduce Charles Dance as Tywin Lannister [in Episode 107]. The scene was a late addition to the script, where Tywin is butchering a stag as he's talking to his son, Jaime. Up to this point you think Jaime is the most despicable person you've ever seen on TV, but when you meet his father, suddenly you understand how he came to be this way. It's an

incredibly tender scene between two monstrous men juxtaposed against the bloody evisceration of that stag. It may be one of my favorite scenes I got to shoot on the show.

CHARLES DANCE: I enjoyed my first scene. It's one of those scenes that are a delight to play because one is concentrating on one thing whilst speaking about something completely different. And I learned a bit of butchery—I like learning something new!

DAVID BENIOFF: A strange thing happened midway through shooting the first season. We realized several of the episodes were coming in with short running times, which meant we had to come up with a slew of new scenes. Unfortunately, our budget was also coming up short, which meant these new scenes generally had to be two-handers, shot interior, without action or VFX or horses or anything, really, but two actors and some dialogue. We loved it. The new directive meant we could write character scenes for our remarkable actors. Since these scenes had not been part of the original outline for the season, they were not plot-oriented so much as character discoveries. We had the chance to spend more time with some of the players we felt had been shortchanged. And we had the opportunity to introduce Tywin Lannister in a whole new way, talking to his favorite son while skinning a stag. That scene was one of the last we wrote for the show and one of our favorites. Watching Charles in that scene, you'd think he skinned three stags a day. He managed to deliver a riveting, note-perfect performance while gutting a dead beast. After watching that, Dan and I looked at each other. We were both thinking the same thing: "We need more Tywin scenes."

[OPPOSITE] *Charles Dance as Tywin Lannister.*

Cersei Lannister

![Lannister sigil]

"**Everyone who isn't us
is an enemy.**"

—Cersei Lannister

The wife of King Robert and Queen of Westeros, Cersei is beautiful, cunning, and ambitious. Fiercely protective of her children and her own family, she is not afraid to play dirty to advance their interests. Cersei bears no love or affection for her husband—in fact, the love of her life is her twin brother, Jaime, with whom she has had an incestuous relationship since they were young. When Robert dies and her son Joffrey assumes the throne, she is forced to govern with her loathed younger brother, Tyrion, while coping with the increasingly erratic behavior of her son.

[OPPOSITE] *Lena Headey as Queen Cersei Lannister.*

LENA HEADEY: As a mother in real life, I can tell you: it's a sort of unbearable love. You'd literally kill for your child. All the things you'd roll your eyes at before you have one of your own—they're all true. I share that with Cersei. She will do anything—she will kill, and she does, for her children, no matter how crazy and fucked up they turn out to be. Now, Cersei's mistake is she can't really face the truth about Joff. I'm happy to report my beautiful son is nothing like Joffrey!

D. B. WEISS: Lena's approach to Cersei affected our own thinking about the character. Her audition included the scene from Episode 102 where she tells Catelyn about the child she lost herself. Her approach to that scene, the way she invested it with complete emotional truth, it informed the way we wrote Cersei from then on, and it still does.

LENA HEADEY: The chance to fully portray somebody who's so layered and fascinating is quite a rarity. Cersei's life has been very complicated from a young age, and she carries a lot of anger, and a lot of fear and paranoia. Her one piece of sanity is her children.

D. B. WEISS: Beauty, brains, wit, and power are a tall order in one person, but they're what anyone playing Cersei Lannister needs. What ultimately enthralled us about Lena's performance was her approach, which was so beautifully understated and at times quietly funny as hell.

LENA HEADEY: Season one was fun, but you really only see the top layer of Cersei: this icy, controlled, no-nonsense woman. In the second season, it was so thrilling. Every scene I was given I was so excited to do! She's scared of Joffrey, her own child. She's questioning her relationship with Jaime. She's being forced to share her innermost secrets with Tyrion, of all people. I just love it—it's been so juicy. I can really lose myself as an actor.

D. B. WEISS: Lena also manages to suggest the strain and unease that power puts on those who wield it. Cersei is the only one of the Lannister siblings who's truly manning the fort and watching out for the Lannister legacy. Ironically, she's also the one Lannister sibling unable to wield power in a straightforward way because of her sex. Being Cersei Lannister is stressful. The tagline of the series—"You win or you die"—comes from her mouth. No one understands the cost of losing better than she does. Her love for her children is very real, and if she does not remain vigilant, her children will die alongside her.

[ABOVE LEFT] *Brother and sister, sharing a passionate moment.* ❖ [ABOVE RIGHT] *Cersei at Winterfell in season one.*
❖ [OPPOSITE] *Lena Headey as Queen Cersei, about to show the true extent of her power to Littlefinger.*

CERSEI

Green paper
Silk with Embroidered
Birds alighting
(My little Bird)

Gold lion Necklace
(small version given
to Sansa to bring news)

Embroidered
lion on Sleeve

Metal Belt
Based on
lannister
Armour.

Metal neck cuff
with long metal
& Jewels

Red Silk with
Red & Gold
Arms.
Gold Metallic
Gauge to
line

COSTUMING CERSEI

[opposite and above] *Cersei costume concept drawings.* ◆ [top right] *Cersei, dressed for the cold Winterfell weather.* ◆ [middle and bottom right] *Two "southern" gowns for the Queen in season two.*

MICHELE CLAPTON: When we first meet Cersei, she's in a deeply unhappy marriage but is set in her ways and her style. Then Robert dies and Joffrey takes power, and slowly she gets harder. The bird embroidered on her clothes gives way to more and more lions. I wanted to increase her shell, I guess. Everything's more ornate, grander, until we finally see her in Episode 209 in a sort of armored corset. I don't know how strong she is really, but she wants to project that image. I've always wanted to do this with her costume, from the start, back when we were doing the pilot. ॐ

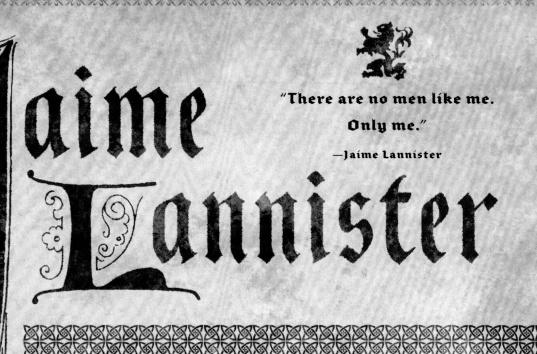

Jaime Lannister

"There are no men like me.

Only me."

—Jaime Lannister

The twin brother (and lover) of Cersei Lannister, Jaime is known as "The Kingslayer," as it was he who killed the usurped King Aerys (whom he had previously sworn to honor and protect). A member of Robert's Kingsguard, Jaime is as beautiful and ruthless as his sister, but less calculating. At the start of the war, he is taken prisoner by Robb Stark's forces.

D. B. WEISS: Many people came in for Jaime, and some of them were very good actors and good-looking guys besides, but when we really looked at them we couldn't help but think: "You're not the most handsome guy in Westeros." And the one or two who did pass muster on that score did a lot of cocky eyebrow wagging and mustache twirling.

What Nikolaj does, over and above being handsome, is to dig beneath Jaime's surface to hit the bedrock of what truly drives him: his love for his sister and, perhaps most of all, his anger at what he perceives to be the unfairness of his situation. All indicators pointed toward a charmed life for him and the adoration of the masses. Now he is reviled for breaking his Kingsguard oath and murdering King Aerys during the rebellion. . . . Never mind that Aerys was quite possibly the worst man in the history of the kingdoms.

NIKOLAJ COSTER-WALDAU (Jaime Lannister): A character like this in a movie—you'd have to put across the nastiness of him in the first ten minutes. But developing the character over the course of a series, to

have more time, it's fun and so rewarding. What I love about this show in general is that it constantly questions preconceived ideas of all the characters.

What I like about Jaime, what I find intriguing about him, is that he actually has a moral code. He's brutal when he has to be, and his morals might not fit with those of others, but they're his. Jaime doesn't apologize for who he is. He's painfully aware of his predicament—he's fallen for his own sister. She's the most important thing in his life. Obviously, that creates some problems for him.

D. B. WEISS: We spent a lot of time with Nik and Lena discussing the Lannister twins' situation. By the time we were done with these discussions, we all realized that, if you were Jaime and Cersei and your experiences were the same as their experiences, you, too, would push a ten-year-old boy out a window. There was something both comforting and terrifying about this realization, something that cuts to the core of why George's books hooked us in the first place. There aren't good guys and bad guys. There are just people pursuing their own interests, as they see them, and their own versions of the good, as they see it. Which is exactly what we all do every day.

[OPPOSITE] *Nikolaj Coster-Waldau as Jaime Lannister.*

NED VS. JAIME

AT THE CONCLUSION OF EPISODE 105, THE LONG-RUNNING TENSION BREWING BETWEEN HOUSES STARK AND LANNISTER FINALLY BOILS OVER WHEN JAIME LANNISTER ATTACKS NED STARK AND HIS MEN IN THE STREETS OF KING'S LANDING. IN THE ENSUING BATTLE, NED IS GRAVELY WOUNDED AND HIS LOYAL RIGHT-HAND MAN JORY CASSEL (PLAYED BY JAMIE SIVES) IS KILLED.

NIKOLAJ COSTER-WALDAU: I absolutely loved the sword fight with Sean. Trouble was brewing between these two characters from their first scene together in the pilot, and this is where they finally faced off. This kind of scene—riding into the square, taking him on, stabbing Jory Cassel in the eye—it awakens the kid inside you.

BRIAN KIRK *(director)*: There was an enormous amount of technical satisfaction in the making of *Game of Thrones*. The large-scale fight sequences, such as the key Ned-Jaime fight, are probably the best examples of this. They demanded painstaking planning and brave execution. The process

[above] *Ser Jaime Lannister, drawn and ready.* ◆ [opposite] *Jaime and Ned face off on location in Malta.*

involved storyboarding the action, tailoring the sets to fit, intense stunt rehearsals—which were themselves filmed and edited by the wonderful [stunt coordinator] Paul Jennings—reviewing and revising the action, integrating special effects, and adding prosthetics for wounds. All of which had to be harnessed to the characters, the story, and the world rather than taking them over.

DAVID BENIOFF: Nikolaj's athleticism came in handy here. He did most of the stunt fighting himself, meaning we didn't have to double him often. And he's quite skilled at jumping on and off a horse. On one take, at the end of the scene, he leaped onto his horse and the horse freaked out, probably because Jaime's scabbard slapped its side. The horse galloped down the street and nearly stomped on a few dead bodies—actually living stuntmen who almost became dead bodies. Nik had to duck as his horse tried to slam him into the side of the alleyway. I believe that take is in the cut, as it looked appropriately dangerous. 🕊

DAVID BENIOFF: Killing Jory was a significant moment for us — his death signals the onset of war between the Starks and the Lannisters. We had become very fond of Jory as interpreted by Jamie Sives, though he didn't have a great deal of screen time. So we spent a lot of time rehearsing the Kingslayer's dagger going into Jory's eyeball.

Tyrion Lannister

"I was born lucky."

—Tyrion Lannister

The third and youngest child of Tywin Lannister, Tyrion has been scorned, derided, and underestimated all his life due to his being born a dwarf—indeed, he is known far and wide as "The Imp." His intelligence and good humor have helped him weather many hardships, with a little help from wine and whores. Having lived most of his life decidedly outside the Game of Thrones, he becomes an unwitting player when he is falsely accused of murder and put on trial, an event that soon leads to all-out civil war. Then, in the wake of Ned Stark's death, Tyrion is appointed to the office of Hand of the King.

[OPPOSITE] Peter Dinklage as Tyrion Lannister. ❖ [NEXT SPREAD LEFT] Tyrion, armed only with a shield, in his first battle. ❖ [NEXT SPREAD RIGHT] Falsely accused of murder, Tyrion admires his view from the sky cell.

PETER DINKLAGE: Tyrion is a survivor. Flawed. Romantic. A contradiction at times. Oftentimes characters in fantasy-themed books or films have only one dimension. Good or bad. Peaceful or violent. The characters [in *Game of Thrones*] burn off the pages because they can be all these things. What better way to have the luxury of exploring a complex character like Tyrion than over the course of ten hours a season? Taking on the role was an easy decision to make.

D. B. WEISS: From the moment Tyrion appeared in the book, we knew we'd need Peter Dinklage to make this show work the way we wanted it to work. So we met him and basically offered him the role off the bat. Having just come off the *Narnia* movie, he wanted us to promise him that he wouldn't have to wear a fake beard longer than six inches. We said we could promise him this . . . and sure enough, he signed on. Peter joining the show was a major milestone for us, a big step away from the show's "Don't quit your day job" beginnings toward reality.

PETER DINKLAGE: For someone who has been treated quite poorly by his family and the world around him, Tyrion really does enjoy his life. At first glance you would think he was a cynic, but he's really not, in my opinion. Intelligence is often mistaken for cynicism. He burns very brightly. He can be quite the asshole at times, but I believe he has a very good heart. And, of course, with the intelligence comes a great sense of humor. It has helped him survive. He embraces who he is, makes fun of himself before you are given a chance to—beating you at your own game. The smartest people I know are also the funniest. He is that.

D. B. WEISS: Tyrion is so many people's favorite character, in the show and the books. He makes people laugh, and that is certainly part of it, but I think it's also because he has the most modern sensibility in many ways. He's not a winking anachronism—he's a product of his world—but he's a skeptic by nature. He understands other people's perspectives, even, or especially, the people he's up against. Though he may try to cover it up with cynicism, this quality speaks to a deep empathy—especially with, as he puts it in George's great phrase, "cripples, bastards, and broken things."

PETER DINKLAGE: Season one seemed to have a number of scenes in which Tyrion is talking himself out of being killed. I loved those scenes. He's always one step ahead of anything that is thrown at him, and he deals with it with humor and oftentimes makes the other party feel like they got the better end of the deal. Fun stuff. But he's much more in his element in season two. He is back at King's Landing doing what he does best: working the

strings of those around him. Not in any Machiavellian way, but to make the system work. And it does. He keeps his enemies closer. He relieves the repugnant King Joffrey of any real damage he can cause. And having been the outsider for so long, he surprises himself with how much he loves playing the insider's game.

I really enjoy the one-on-one scenes. Nothing makes me happier being an actor than working with someone like Lena Headey, for example, and finding things you never knew were there when you first read it.

LENA HEADEY: I love working with Peter, as we've been good friends for years. The Tyrion/Cersei relationship is fascinating to me. Safety and generosity is very important when working on such intense material, and you have that with Pete in abundance, so it's really exciting. It's such an odd relationship. . . . I think there's an intense loyalty within it somewhere.

PETER DINKLAGE: The four people in the ring with Tyrion on the show are mainly Cersei, Bronn, Varys, and Shae. Each relationship is so unique from one another and equally important in many ways. The mold is broken on a few of them—breaking your expectations on what you thought the relationship was, where it was headed. It also helps to have brilliant and fun friends to play with in Lena, Conleth Hill, Jerome Flynn, and Sibel Kekilli. They all make me a better actor.

D. B. WEISS: It takes a lot of craft to play Tyrion. The story, and his backstory, involve a tremendous range of experiences and emotions, and Peter has to convey them all behind the humor and detachment that Tyrion wears like armor. I don't have to go into too much detail about the kind of job he did—the Emmy he won [for Outstanding Supporting Actor] makes a lot of what I have to say redundant. As good as he was in the first season, he's better in the second, I think. He's someone you want to watch at work. And he's someone you want to drink beer with. Which is good, because we're all going to be working and drinking beer in Belfast and Croatia with him for as long as the show lasts. And if it lasts a long time, it will be in large part because of Peter.

HOUSE BARATHEON
A BRIEF HISTORY

"I will kill every Targaryen I get my hands on."
—Robert Baratheon

House Baratheon was born in the Wars of Conquest, when Aegon Targaryen invaded the Seven Kingdoms, and is the youngest of the Great Houses of Westeros. Its founder, Orys Baratheon, was a commander in Aegon's army and, according to rumor, Aegon's half brother. Aegon entrusted Orys with securing Storm's End, a stronghold that had never been taken by force.

When Argilac the Arrogant, the last of the Storm Kings, foolishly left the safety of Storm's End to meet Orys in open battle, Argilac was soundly defeated. Orys was awarded Argilac's lands, his holdings . . . and his daughter.

House Baratheon's loyalty to the crown was broken when the crown prince, Rhaegar Targaryen, abducted Lyanna Stark, the betrothed of Robert Baratheon. This set off a chain of events that led Robert to rebel against Rhaegar and his father, "Mad King" Aerys. With the initial support of Houses Stark, Tully, and Arryn, and eventually of Lannister, Robert was victorious.

Upon taking the crown, Robert ruled over the Seven Kingdoms as the Targaryens had: from atop the Iron Throne. His younger brother Stannis was given the former Targaryen stronghold of Dragonstone, while his youngest brother, Renly, became lord of Storm's End. Following King Robert's death in a hunting accident, both brothers openly challenged Robert's son and heir, Prince Joffrey, each declaring themselves to the rightful king of Westeros.

GENDRY
(a bastard)

JOFFREY
BARATHEON

MYRCELLA
BARATHEON

TOMMEN
BARATHEON

ROBERT
BARATHEON

CERSEI
(LANNISTER)
BARATHEON

STANNIS
BARATHEON

RENLY
BARATHEON

HOUSE BARATHEON

SEAT:
Storm's End,
King's Landing,
Dragonstone

SIGIL:
A Crowned
Black Stag

"Ours Is the Fury!"

Robert Baratheon

Known to some as the "Usurper," Robert Baratheon led the rebellion that overthrew the powerful Targaryen dynasty. He was crowned king but proved to be a less effective ruler than he was a warrior, being more interested in whoring and drinking than affairs of state. He eventually met his end from a wound sustained in a boar hunt, leaving the Seven Kingdoms in turmoil.

D. B. WEISS: The very first casting video I watched for *Game of Thrones* was Mark Addy's audition for Robert Baratheon. After the first take, I thought, "This casting process is going to be easy! The very first guy I see is the perfect embodiment of the character he's playing. I guess people will just read the script and get it." Alas, my optimism was unfounded.

We did, however, get Mark. Up to that point, he'd been known—to me, anyway—mostly for comic roles. He is indeed a very funny man, but he packed in so much sadness, pathos, and rage behind Robert's forced mirth, it was masterly work.

MARK ADDY (*Robert Baratheon*): Robert was meant to be a warrior, not to rule. I hooked into the idea that being all-powerful and in charge is not a bed of roses. Robert has to deal with all the mundane shit of governing, the minutiae of running the Seven Kingdoms, and he's terrible at it, frankly. He needs Ned to come rescue him. I enjoyed playing those scenes with Sean, from the crypt scene in the pilot to Robert's final deathbed scene [in Episode 107].

SEAN BEAN (*Ned Stark*): Mark and I were at the Royal Academy of Dramatic Art at the same time, and we're both from Yorkshire, so we got on quite well. I think it helped especially with that

> "I'm not trying to honor you. I'm trying to get you to run my kingdom while I eat, drink, and whore my way to an early grave."
>
> **—Robert Baratheon**

particular scene on the Kingsroad where we talk about old times [in Episode 102]. I think it comes across on-screen that we're old friends.

TIM VAN PATTEN (*director, season one*): Sean and Mark had a beautiful shorthand between them, and watching them play off each other was a joy. You could really feel their kinship and the full weight of their history when they were together. It was obvious that these were two old warriors with a lifetime of pain, suffering, and struggle between them. Yet when it called for a lighter moment, they could hit it so subtly and with such grace. How they acknowledged the changing tide of their world was beautiful.

MARK ADDY: Of course, the other key to Robert's story is his miserable marriage to Cersei and the love he lost. One of best times I had on *Game of Thrones* was doing that scene [in Episode 105] between Robert and Cersei, where they look back on their marriage. It came in at the very last minute—seven pages of dialogue! It was fantastic stuff to play, and to have the opportunity to do a scene with Lena that wasn't "Shut up, woman!" was wonderful. It allowed the audience to learn so much about the two of them and their history, all in one scene.

[OPPOSITE AND ABOVE] *Mark Addy as King Robert Baratheon.*

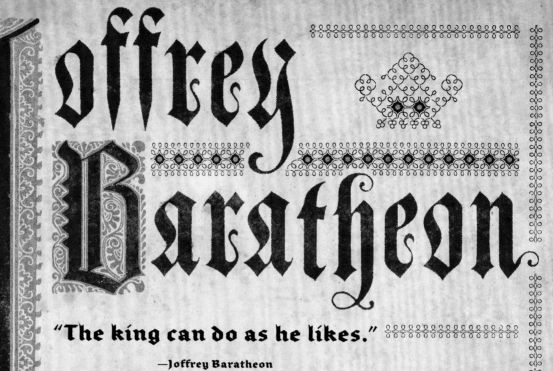

Joffrey Baratheon

"The king can do as he likes."

—Joffrey Baratheon

The son of Robert Baratheon and Cersei Lannister, Joffrey is betrothed to Sansa Stark. He appears courteous and gallant at first, but soon reveals himself to be spoiled, violent, and cruel. He has spent his childhood under the close protection and tutelage of his mother but is starting to come into his own as he attains more power. He proves to be a dangerous and unstable ruler when he is crowned king in the wake of his father's untimely death— abruptly ordering the execution of Ned Stark against his mother's wishes.

D. B. WEISS: Jack Gleeson is a real actor—because he's one of the nicest, most polite, most intelligent people you could ever want to meet, and yet he portrays a budding psychopath with chilling believability.

JACK GLEESON: For some reason, for me, playing the bad guy is so much fun. I remember I was shooting the riot scene from Episode 206, raging and screaming and being a brat, with horse shit all over my face. And [director] David Nutter said to me, "It's the kind of character you can't just put on, that you've got to reach into your soul to pull it off." So I don't know if I should be worried! I hope there's no Joffrey lurking within me. . . .

Robert's deathbed. That scene [in Episode 107] was revelatory for me. The idea that Joff is just a kid who wanted a

dad and never had one. All Joff wants is some validation, some kind of "I love you." Instead he's rejected so obviously and publicly—it's not a surprise that it motivates him to hate other people, to abuse other people. I remember [director] Dan Minahan really opened my mind to the idea that the stuff Joffrey does really isn't his fault. He spoke about the idea that he might really like Sansa deep down, but his only role models are Robert and Cersei and he feels he has to act a certain way. He's a product of his circumstance.

Joffrey starts the series as a bratty child, but he grows into something much darker. I don't think he's capable of chopping off Ned's head in the first episode. That comes with power and from the anger and sense of loss after his own father has died. And it gets worse in season two. Much worse.

NED'S EXECUTION

EPISODE 109: "BAELOR"

WITHOUT QUESTION, THE MOST BUZZED-ABOUT SCENE IN SEASON ONE OF GAME OF THRONES *WAS THE SHOCKING DEATH OF* NED STARK, *EXECUTED IN FULL VIEW OF HIS TWO DAUGHTERS ON THE COMMAND OF THE RUTHLESS BOY KING,* JOFFREY BARATHEON. *THIS PIVOTAL SCENE PROVED TO BE A UNIQUELY REWARDING EXPERIENCE FOR THE CAST AND CREW.*

DAVID BENIOFF: For us, from the very beginning of our preparations for the series, we knew season one would climax with two critical scenes: Ned Stark's beheading and the birth of Dany's dragons. Those scenes conclude the final two episodes of the season and mark a turning point for the entire story. In the case of the execution, Ned's death signals a decidedly darker turn for the tale. Our intrepid hero, trying desperately to protect his family and preserve his honor in a dishonorable place, fails at both. Courage and honesty are not enough to prevail in a dangerous world.

SEAN BEAN: It was tough for me during interviews [promoting the show]. I couldn't very well say, "Well, Ned gets his head chopped off in the ninth episode."

DAVID BENIOFF: We were very lucky to have Alan Taylor directing. And we were very lucky to have Sean Bean playing Ned Stark.

From the early chapters of *A Game of Thrones*, Sean's face was the one I pictured in the role. He has a quality few actors possess: the ability to convey all the weight of a very hard life without saying anything at all. A lifetime of war and mourning left Ned a somber, quiet man, but he was still a family man, devoted to his wife and his children. He was a man you would trust with your life. He was *not* a man you kill in the first season of a series most people didn't think would ever get made.

ALAN TAYLOR (*director*): There was really only one fort in Malta that was big enough to accommodate the scene, but when [director of photography] Alik Sakharov and I got there, our shoulders drooped because the sun was always in the wrong place. If you shot one way, you saw a modern city, but if you shot the other way, the sun was flattening everything. So Alik and I designed the shoot in such a way that we could basically chase the sun.

ALIK SAKHAROV (*director of photography*): We ended up shooting completely out of sequence, shooting around the square, all these different elements as the sun was rotating. Alan knew specifically shot for shot, setup for setup, what he wanted to do, so in the end, it all pieced together beautifully. It's a seamless sequence and it's all Alan.

DAVID BENIOFF: We see much of the execution through Arya's eyes. We wanted the audience to believe what Arya believes: there must be a way to rescue Ned. The plucky little girl will somehow fight her way through the crowd and save Ned with the help of Needle, her castle-forged sword. We wanted the audience to think, "There's no way they're gonna let Ned Stark die. He's the hero of the whole show."

SOPHIE TURNER (*Sansa Stark*): This scene was one of the most upsetting scenes I had to film. I remember the first take, when I was screaming for Joffrey to stop, I began to cry without even intending to do so. The two-hundred-plus extras shouting "Traitor!" at Sean added to the high emotions of that scene.

MAISIE WILLIAMS (*Arya Stark*): All those one-on-one scenes I had with Sean over the course of season one really did help when we shot the beheading—which was one of the last scenes I had with him. Arya's whole world ends in this scene, watching her father go. She can't trust her sister, she doesn't know how to get in touch with her brothers, and her mother—whom she's never been very close to—isn't with her. She's truly alone.

SEAN BEAN: In the end, what the scene, what his death, is about: keeping his daughters safe. He gives the false confession to protect Sansa, sealing his fate, but he also spends his final moments protecting Arya. He sees her out on that statue of Baelor and alerts Yoren—"Get her out of here," basically. I quite liked that moment at the end when he looks up to the statue and sees she's gone.

ALAN TAYLOR: One of the last shots I put in was the shot of Ned seeing that Arya's not on the statue anymore, and it turned out to be one of the most emotionally satisfying moments in the scene.

We definitively finish on Ned's POV when his head comes off, so that in those final beats we shift from his POV to Arya's, cutting to her watching the flock of birds overhead. It's a way of saying that, from now on, the story's going to be told through different eyes; it's been passed on. You hear his breathing, it's silenced, then you shift to hers.

FRANK DOELGER (*producer*): The challenge going forward is "What do you do without Ned?" What's interesting about the story is that Ned's death, and Robert's death, have left a very serious power vacuum, and you have a ton of contenders to fill it. It'll be fun for the viewers to see which characters start emerging and moving to the center. No one expected Ned to go, but the game continues, and no one's safe.

DAVID BENIOFF: **Ned's execution was the scene in the novel where I knew, finally and irrevocably, that George was playing for keeps. Commuting Ned's sentence in the show would have been a betrayal of everything we love about the books. When people ask us, "Did you ever think about keeping Ned alive?" The answer is no. The Lord of Winterfell had to die.**

[opposite] *On location at Fort Manoel in Malta.* ♦ [top] *Maisie Williams as Arya Stark, watching the horror unfold from the statue of Baelor the Blessed.* ♦ [above] *Prepping Ned's beheading.* ♦ [following four pages] *Ned Stark's final moments.*

ALAN TAYLOR: There's been such a wonderful cultural response to Ned's death. It made me really appreciate the fans of the book; they were really great about keeping it a secret. It's cool when the fans are on your side. It was exciting and daring to kill him off, but then you approach season two and all you're thinking is "Oh, no! He's been killed off." And my initial feeling was "We need someone to fill his shoes." But that's not the way to go. You can't fill his shoes, and that ends up being the point.

GEORGE R. R. MARTIN: It's funny when you get this huge reaction to Ned's death. Ned was *always* marked for death, so the kids could come into their own. As long as Daddy is around, the kids are going to live in Daddy's shadow, but once you remove him, then you have a lot more tension. But I didn't want to remove him too soon, so I kept him around a long time so you get really invested in him. So when he's lost, it's a tremendous blow.

"Courage and honesty
are not enough to prevail in
a dangerous world."

— DAVID BENIOFF

Renly Baratheon

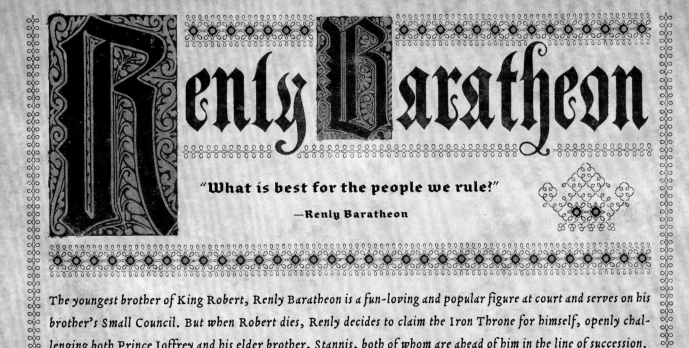

> ### "What is best for the people we rule?"
> —Renly Baratheon

The youngest brother of King Robert, Renly Baratheon is a fun-loving and popular figure at court and serves on his brother's Small Council. But when Robert dies, Renly decides to claim the Iron Throne for himself, openly challenging both Prince Joffrey and his elder brother, Stannis, both of whom are ahead of him in the line of succession.

GETHIN ANTHONY (*Renly Baratheon*): The best description of Renly, funnily enough, is given by George R. R. Martin in the novels, when he describes him as enjoying food and wine but is neither a glutton nor a drunkard, and that he can converse with high- and lowborn alike. What is interesting about Renly's journey in the series is that we see him progress from courtier to king. The way he moves through the different corridors of power changes, and that arc, was really exciting to explore.

MARGAERY and LORAS TYRELL

When Renly Baratheon declares himself king, he does so with the support of the powerful House Tyrell of Highgarden, an alliance sealed in marriage to the beautiful and shrewd Margaery Tyrell. Margaery's brother, Ser Loras Tyrell, is known far and wide and the Knight of the Flowers and is Renly's most loyal follower . . . as well as his secret lover.

MICHELE CLAPTON: Margaery Tyrell [played by Natalie Dormer] sweeps into King's Landing and takes it by storm. As such, her wardrobe is very unique and very much at odds with everything else in King's Landing. It's a very structured look—the new style coming in after the war. For the first time in a long time, Cersei won't be the trendsetter in the capital. It's a fun way to reflect their future rivalry.

GETHIN ANTHONY: I had an absolutely fantastic time working with Finn Jones [who plays Loras Tyrell], and I was very excited that the relationship between Renly and Loras was given some story time. The series has an opportunity to tell George's stories in an enhanced way when you get to see the perspective of characters who are not POV characters in the book. A prime example is the Renly-Loras relationship.

[ABOVE] *Natalie Dormer as Margaery Tyrell and Finn Jones as Loras Tyrell.* ❖ [OPPOSITE] *Gethin Anthony as Renly Baratheon.*

> "Must be strange for you... a man from another land, despised by most, feared by all... But you carry on, whispering in one king's ear, and then the next. I admire you."
>
> —Littlefinger to Varys

· MASTER ·

of COINS

LITTLEFINGER
(PETYR BAELISH)

Lord Petyr Baelish, a master of court intrigue, is often called "Littlefinger" and serves as the Master of Coin on Robert's Small Council. While of noble blood, he comes from a relatively poor family and has managed to rise high due to his brilliance, ambition, and unscrupulous nature. He grew up as a foster brother to Catelyn Stark and harbors an unrequited love for her, having fought (and lost) a duel for her hand.

· MASTER ·

of WHISPERS

"And I admire you, Lord Baelish. A grasper from a minor house with a major talent for befriending powerful men. And women."

—Varys to Littlefinger

VARYS

A clever and enigmatic eunuch with a mysterious past, Varys serves the Small Council as the king's spymaster, or "Master of Whispers." Behaving in an obsequious manner that masks his true motives, he is liked by few and trusted by fewer. Varys makes it his business to know everybody else's and affectionately refers to his spies as his "little birds." He engages in a friendly rivalry with the court's other spymaster, Lord Petyr Baelish, a.k.a. "Littlefinger."

AIDAN GILLEN (*Littlefinger*): Littlefinger's always a step or two ahead of most people and revels in the uncertainty he provokes; it's a perfect stage for his schemes within schemes. You're never really certain whose side he's on, which of course is how he likes it. And the lovely thing is that it's all rooted in rejection, romantically and otherwise. Without Catelyn's passing him over way back when, he wouldn't be half as driven as he is—he has a lot to be grateful to her for. Rejection can be a great stimulus, and Littlefinger will never, ever let himself be pushed to the side again. This is where we might see a crack of vulnerability because, no matter what resolutions he's made, there's still strong feeling there.

DAVID BENIOFF: We first noticed Aidan Gillen on *The Wire*, playing an idealistic mayoral candidate. He wasn't just good; he was captivating. And I had no idea he was Irish. In the books, Petyr Baelish [a.k.a. "Littlefinger"] is quite short, and Aidan is not short. But we made a decision early in the casting process: let's always cast the best actor for the role, regardless of whether he or she matches the description in the books. Aidan is the best possible actor for Littlefinger. At this point, I can't imagine anyone else in the role.

CONLETH HILL (*Varys*): The key to Varys is that he's one way in public, when he's working, very fey, giggly, and effete for want of a better word, but there are moments when

CONLETH HILL: I think both Varys and Littlefinger enjoy their rivalry. Littlefinger's ambition is a bit more obvious than Varys's. And I think Littlefinger finds the eunuch intriguing. He's trying to figure him out. The most physical scene I've had to do is walking the length of the throne room with Littlefinger. I'm lucky I don't have to ride a horse.

he drops all that and speaks honestly. That stuff is great to play. When Ned asks Varys whom he truly serves, and Varys answers, "The realm," I think that's true. There's a moral code there. Now, what he does in service of this code is often questionable, but I think that's the beauty of it.

Ned Stark, to Varys, was a good man and an honorable man. But Varys relates to Tyrion, as they've both been outcasts at one time or another. He sees in Tyrion someone who plays the game well, and Varys loves playing the game. Ned was too honorable and too good—he disdained the game.

DAVID BENIOFF: Sean Bean is a quiet man. I didn't see him laugh on set that many times, but in 99 percent of those

occasions, it was Conleth Hill triggering the laughter. Conleth isn't just funny—he's wicked funny.

D. B. WEISS: Conleth even plays the broader aspects of Varys's public persona subtly, which is a hard thing to do. And when it comes time for him to drop the mask and talk straight, he effortlessly turns on a dime. I love watching him work, especially with Peter [Dinklage] and Aidan.

[OPPOSITE] *The Master of Whispers.* ❖ [BELOW] *The Master of Coin.* ❖ [PREVIOUS SPREAD] *Aidan Gillen as Littlefinger, and Conleth Hill as Varys.*

AIDAN GILLEN: Varys and Littlefinger's sparring is fun and razor-sharp. Either of these two would ice the other without a second thought, if need be, which would be a shame because they're a good match for each other. The world would be a duller place. Of course, this won't happen anytime soon. Spy versus spy is always good.

BRIENNE of TARTH

The only child of Lord Selwyn of Tarth, the unusually tall Brienne (Gwendoline Christie) rejected the courtly life of a lady, growing into a strong and formidable warrior, though she is mocked by her peers—her nickname is "Brienne the Beauty." She swears herself to the would-be king Renly Baratheon and later finds herself in the service of Catelyn Stark, who greatly respects her for her skill in battle and unwavering loyalty.

GWENDOLINE CHRISTIE (Brienne): Emotionally I can completely connect to Brienne's feelings of isolation due to her physical size and the abuse that she suffers from others due to her appearance. I relished the opportunity to bring to life this woman who is marginalized simply because she does not conform to social norms and conventions of beauty and who has overcome her vulnerability with physical strength and skill in swordsmanship and battle equal to that of any man.

BRONN

The sellsword Bronn (Jerome Flynn) finds himself in the right place at the right time when Tyrion Lannister is taken prisoner by Catelyn Stark and accused of murder. Bronn seizes the opportunity, successfully defends Tyrion in a trial by combat, and quickly becomes his indispensable right-hand man.

JEROME FLYNN (Bronn): I tend to be cast quite a lot as a "good guy," but I enjoy playing characters with a bit more darkness in them. I love the mystery about Bronn—you never know where you stand with him. And I like the fact that he's working his way up in the world, ad-libbing his way through the story and taking opportunities as they come.

I think Bronn enjoys Tyrion. He's drawn to him as a fellow outsider and admires his cunning and intelligence. If Bronn has any friends, I think Tyrion is his closest—but it doesn't mean loyalty.

[ABOVE AND BELOW] *Jerome Flynn as Bronn.* ❖ [OPPOSITE] *Gwendoline Christie as Brienne of Tarth.*

BATTLE OF THE BLACKWATER

EPISODE 209: "BLACKWATER"

IN THE NINTH EPISODE OF SEASON TWO, STANNIS BARATHEON (STEPHEN DILLANE) ATTACKS KING'S LANDING WITH HIS POWERFUL NAVAL FLEET IN AN ATTEMPT TO CLAIM THE IRON THRONE FOR HIMSELF. GROSSLY OUTNUMBERED, HAND OF THE KING TYRION LANNISTER (PETER DINKLAGE) MUST DEFEND THE CITY. A MASSIVE ACTION SET PIECE SHOWN FROM MULTIPLE POINTS OF VIEW, THE "BATTLE OF THE BLACKWATER" SEQUENCE IS THE MAJOR CLIMAX OF SEASON TWO, AND IT PROVED TO BE A HUGE CHALLENGE FOR THE PRODUCTION TEAM, BOTH IN CONCEPTION AND EXECUTION.

GEORGE R. R. MARTIN: I conceived the battle of the Blackwater simply because I wanted a big cool battle. One of my pet peeves with movie battles is how they're often depicted. Battles are about the geography, the lay of the land, who takes the high ground . . . tactics, strategy, and thought. But in a movie, it's usually two armies lined up on opposite sides of the field and running at each other, which is idiotic. My intent in creating the Blackwater battle was showing it working on several levels—Tyrion's thought going into it. How does he face a larger army and a large fleet? What can he do to try to hold the city? And of course, shifting

[above] *Tyrion and his faithful squire Podrick Payne (Daniel Portman).* ♦ [opposite] *Tyrion in battle.* ♦ [following spread] *Stannis Baratheon's troops storm the beach.*

❧

back and forth from his defense of the city to Davos Seaworth and Stannis on the opposing side.

NEIL MARSHALL (*director*): The challenges of staging a massive battle like this, especially on a TV show—which as far as I know is virtually unheard of—are twofold.

First, and this goes for pretty much every film I've done before, there's never enough time or money. You're always up against the clock and struggling to make your resources stretch in order to both tell the story and get as much production value on-screen as possible. This is just a fact of life, and you have to deal with it. The second part is about how you deal with it. You have to think big, but you also have to think fast, and on a film set, those two things are more often than not incompatible. But I've done a few large-scale sequences now, including a huge battle in my last movie [*Centurion*], which we shot in just three days, so I've learned to think on my feet.

The same problems existed here—how do I make a few hundred men look like a hundred thousand? Well, first of all, even if we had a hundred thousand men, we'd still have to focus on the central characters and their story, so we might only see the full scale of the battle for a few establishing shots. I can achieve these shots using VFX, so I know I can achieve the scale.

The rest is all about making sure that every single extra, prop, explosion, fireball, or anything else we want in the shot actually gets in front of the camera. Anything else would be a waste. So I use long lenses to compact the image and pack everyone we have in front of the camera. This makes the action look dense and fierce, and it makes the audience think

D. B. WEISS: Neil's facility and innovation with action, fighting, and suspense are incredible. We were in cutting mode on the battle, taking beats out of the sequence because we thought they wouldn't be achievable. Then Neil showed up, and the first thing he did was to start asking us to put new stuff in—"What if we did this? . . . What if we did that? . . . What if they used the boat this way, and they made their way to these battlements, and all these guys caught fire and got smashed by giant rocks?" And he got it all.

that there must be similar amounts of people on either side that they just can't see. It's a simple trick and it works. And it's just one of many.

For me it's about being selective. Getting the shots you know you are going to use. I have the advantage of having been an editor for eight years before I directed my

first feature. It's a skill that comes in very handy when you've got an hour left to get three setups and you figure out a way of shooting all of them in one setup, knowing you can later cut into it and make it look like you got all three. So much of what we do is an illusion, so I use every trick up my sleeve to pull off a battle sequence like this.

INSIDE HBO's GAME OF THRONES

Rory McCann as Sandor Clegane, or the Hound, Joffrey's ruthless personal bodyguard with a soft spot for his liege's fiancée, Sansa Stark.

LIAM CUNNINGHAM (*Davos Seaworth*): It's incredibly technical working on an episode like this. Thankfully, I had a shorthand with Neil, having worked with him before [on the films *Dog Soldiers* and *Centurion*]. We work together by nods and winks and such. It was fun. The VFX team would bring up the laptop with the animated storyboard to show me exactly what the shot was going to be, so I could position myself. It's fun to shoot these action sequences—it's visual storytelling. You have to really understand, as an actor, where the character's mind is at in any given moment to keep it grounded. I love how subjective the episode is—it's all rooted in character. You see the entire episode through the eyes of Davos, Sansa, and Tyrion. It's edge-of-the-seat stuff, fantastic storytelling. 🙠

[opposite and far right] *Concept art for the battle of the Blackwater.* ✦ [above left] *Shooting the carnage.* ✦ [left] *The massive ship set at the Linen Mill Studios.*

IV Westeros

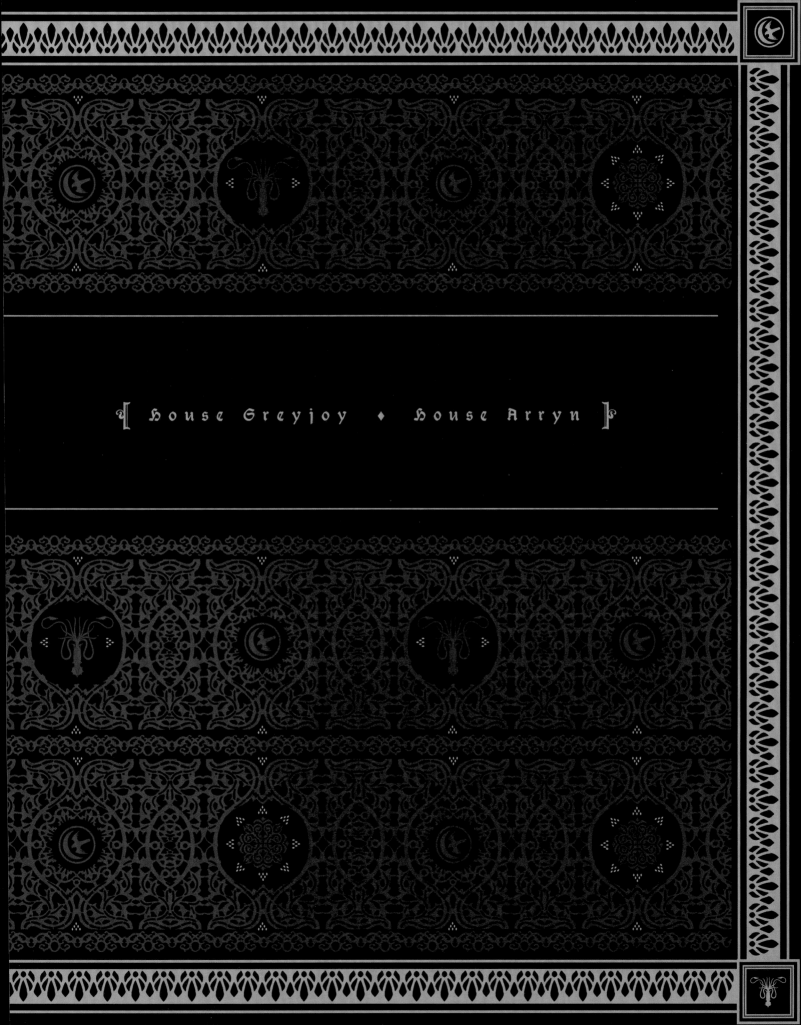

[House Greyjoy ◆ House Arryn]

THE IRON ISLANDS
HOUSE GREYJOY
A BRIEF HISTORY

"We do not sow. We are Ironborn.
We're not subjects. We're not slaves. We do not plow the field
or toil in the mine. We take what is ours."

—Balon Greyjoy

First settling on the Iron Islands in the days of the First Men, the proud denizens of this rocky archipelago refer to themselves as "Ironborn." Isolated from the peoples and cultures of the mainland, the Ironborn ruled as kings for centuries, worshipping their own unique deity, the Drowned God, and cultivating a lifestyle that celebrates pillaging. Their infamous fleet of longships was unmatched and feared throughout the world, and at the height of their power, the Ironborn controlled most of the western coast and the entirety of what are now the Riverlands.

When Aegon Targaryen conquered Westeros, they lost control of all their mainland holdings, but Aegon allowed the Ironborn to keep the Iron Islands. Vickon of House Greyjoy was installed as the region's lord, provided he pledge fealty to the crown.

The Greyjoys are iron to the core, claiming descent from the mythic Grey King in the Age of Heroes, who was said to have slain the sea dragon Nagga and taken a mermaid as his wife. They believe strongly in the old ways, taking the utmost pride in the Ironborn's ancient reaving culture, embodied in their family motto, "We Do Not Sow." Ruling over the Iron Islands from their stronghold of Pyke, they served the monarchy from a distance, waiting for the right opportunity to break free and rule as kings again.

That opportunity presented itself when Robert Baratheon took the Iron Throne from House Targaryen. House Greyjoy had built up a mighty fleet, and its patriarch,

Balon Greyjoy, seized the moment to try to break free of the Seven Kingdoms. Balon declared his region free and independent and himself its king.

Balon assumed the new king of Westeros, who had a reputation for whoring and excessive drinking, could not muster a force to withstand the Ironborn. In this, he was gravely mistaken. Robert Baratheon answered Balon's rebellion with a host of valiant men from nine of the great houses, including Stark and Lannister. Two of Balon's sons were slain in battle, and the rebellion was crushed.

House Greyjoy surrendered, swearing loyalty to Robert and the Iron Throne. Balon was allowed to keep his title as Lord of the Iron Islands, but he paid a great price. His only surviving son, Theon, a boy of eight, was taken hostage to ensure Balon would not rebel again. Eddard Stark took Theon to Winterfell as his ward and raised him alongside his own sons.

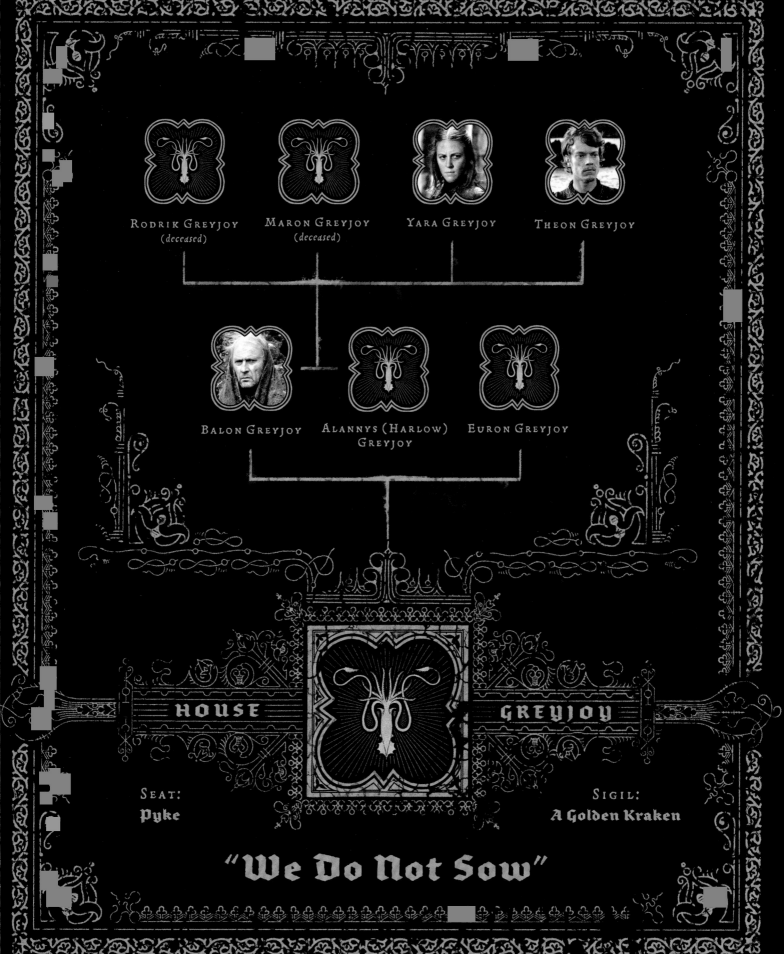

RODRIK GREYJOY
(deceased)

MARON GREYJOY
(deceased)

YARA GREYJOY

THEON GREYJOY

BALON GREYJOY

ALANNYS (HARLOW)
GREYJOY

EURON GREYJOY

HOUSE GREYJOY

SEAT:
Pyke

SIGIL:
A Golden Kraken

"We Do Not Sow"

CREATING PYKE

DAVID BENIOFF (executive producer, writer): Northern Ireland might not have snowy mountains or warm, sunny climates, but if you're looking for rocky, wet, inhospitable islands, you've come to the right country. Robbie Boake, our intrepid locations man, photographed every dramatic, windswept cove in the country. We found the perfect location in Ballintoy Harbor for Pyke's harbor and for the "baptism" scene [in Episode 203] where Theon recommits himself to the faith of the Drowned God. As for the castle of Pyke [an interior set], Gemma Jackson came up with some inspired touches, including a fireplace sculpted in the shape of a great kraken.

[opposite top] *The Lordsport Harbor set, in Northern Ireland.* ✦ [above] *Early concept art, Pyke Castle.* ✦ [opposite bottom] *Concept art, Balon's chamber.* ✦ [next spread] *Balon Greyjoy's chamber, in Pyke Castle.*

❧

GEMMA JACKSON (production designer): I think it works, emotionally, that set. And even if you don't see the tapestries that clearly on-screen, I think it affects things— helps the actors—probably because I come from a theater background.

D. B. WEISS (executive producer, writer): Gemma just made the whole thing seem so damp, and [season two cinematographers] Kramer Morgenthau and P. J. Dillon helped her out with some light-through-water effects. Like Northern Ireland, it feels colder than it is.

MICHELE CLAPTON (costume designer): I think the look for the Iron Islands is my favorite. As we do whenever we're designing a new look for a specific region, we examined their surroundings. In the case of the Iron Islands, it's damp and drafty, rocky, surrounded by sea. So the costumes are wind resistant as opposed to warm—thin, padded linen pieces. We have a lot of armor on this show, so it was important to make each look distinct, so you can identify it immediately

when you see it. Rather than using metal armor, we used riveting and studding, which we would assume is padded behind and therefore pretty resistant to arrows or blades. Then there's a metal breastplate, covered in leather, with the kraken sigil branded on it.

Instead of a cape—we've done so many capes—it's a piece that can be sculpted around the actor, so it becomes windproof; stiff but fluid, too. And Alfie [Allen], in particular, looks great in it—it makes him move in a different way. I didn't want them to have too much ephemeral stuff. Very simple, not particularly cheerful. As for the color, it's the color of the rocks—gray, with some yellowy patches. It works well—and feels very much of the world. ҉

TINA JONES *(set decorator, season two)*: **Pyke's castle was a fun set to do— you can really let your imagination run riot on a show like this. We scattered seashells and seaweed throughout the chamber and found a few pieces of furniture with a bleached look, as if the sea had come in and gone out again. Gemma and [concept artist] Kim Pope came up with concepts for these wonderful tattered tapestries that adorn the walls.** *(see following spread)*

Theon Greyjoy

"Theon . . . did you hate us the whole time?"

—Bran Stark

Heir to Balon Greyjoy of the Iron Islands, Theon grew up as Ned Stark's ward and hostage, forced to live at Winterfell after his father's rebellion was crushed by Ned Stark many years before. Believing he can trust him, Robb Stark sends Theon back to his family to enlist their aid in the war. But Theon's father has a different plan—the Greyjoys will go to war against the North. Torn between his own blood and the family that raised him, Theon chooses blood and betrays the Starks, eventually attacking Winterfell.

D. B. WEISS: Theon is one of my favorite characters, made even more so by the incredible depth of Alfie's portrayal. I love him because he does reprehensible things, but he does them for reasons that resonate with almost everyone: he wants to belong, he wants respect, he wants to be taken seriously by the people who matter to him. Alfie invests every line and look with all these things, and he makes sure we never lose our sympathy with him even as he's heading into darker and darker territory.

ALFIE ALLEN (*Theon Greyjoy*): In the books, Theon is largely in the background until he suddenly comes front and center. In a weird way, life mirrored art in the first season—apart from a few fun scenes, Theon is off to the side while Robb and Jon and everyone else get all the juicy bits. Theon wants to prove himself, and as an actor, I wanted to prove myself. But I always knew what was in store for me in season two, so I had to be patient and just have a great time being part of such a wonderful production, working with so many amazing people.

I think, in the show, much more than in the books, it's a bigger struggle for him, whether or not to betray the Starks. We made a bigger deal out of the brotherly relationship he has with Robb. There's this great scene [in Episode 201] where he tells Robb he wants to avenge Ned's death, and I really think he means it in that moment. But he ends up making a lot of bad choices—not because he's evil. He's just trying to do the right thing all the time and please everyone.

He's been raised by the Starks under one code but comes from a family with an entirely different code. I don't think he really knows how to be Ironborn, to be a Greyjoy. He says he does, wears it like a badge, romanticizes it in his mind, but he doesn't really know what it means . . . and he ends up making a lot of tragic mistakes because of it. He wants so desperately to prove himself to his father and sister that he keeps digging himself deeper and deeper into a hole. There's a scene [in Episode 210] where Maester Luwin tells him, "You're not the man you're pretending to be." And Theon answers, "I've gone too far to pretend to be anything else."

GEMMA WHELAN (*Yara Greyjoy*): Yara is strong, fierce, and proud of who she is and where she comes from, with a glint in her eye and a sharp quip to cut her brother down to size. I have loved researching her and breathing life into the wonderful scripts—wearing her exceptionally empowering, leather thigh-high boots has helped, of course!

[ABOVE] *Gemma Whelan as Yara Greyjoy.* ❖ [OPPOSITE] *Alfie Allen as Theon Greyjoy.* ❖
[NEXT SPREAD] *Theon is baptized by a priest of the Drowned God.*

THE VALE of ARRYN
HOUSE ARRYN
A BRIEF HISTORY

"The Eyrie. They say it's impregnable."

—Tyrion Lannister

"Give me ten good men and some climbing spikes—
I'll impregnate the bitch."

—Bronn

The Arryns of the Vale are one of the oldest and most distinguished families in the Seven Kingdoms. They are direct descendants of the Andal invaders, who sailed from Essos thousands of years ago with weapons of steel to take Westeros from the First Men. Legend tells that Ser Artys Arryn, known as the "Winged Knight," soared through the sky on a giant falcon and battled the Griffin King atop the peak of the highest mountain. Ser Artys's victory ended the line of Mountain Kings and was the first great victory in the Andals' conquest of Westeros. The region was ever after known as the Vale of Arryn.

Thousands of years later, House Arryn submitted when Aegon and his dragons arrived in Westeros. Thus, House Arryn was allowed to maintain its rule over the region as Lords Paramount of the Vale and Wardens of the East.

House Arryn remained loyal to the Targaryen dynasty until "Mad King" Aerys called for the heads of Robert Baratheon and Eddard Stark. Led by Lord Jon Arryn, House Arryn joined with Houses Stark and Baratheon in rebellion, and Lord Jon helped secure the support of the powerful Tully family by taking their youngest daughter, Lysa, as his wife. Upon winning the Iron Throne, Robert named Lord Jon as the Hand of the King,

a position he held until his untimely and mysterious death. His son, Robin, a sickly boy, now rules as Lord of the Vale.

House Arryn's seat, the Eyrie, is a fabled and impregnable fortress. Standing triumphant, high in the snowcapped peaks of the Mountains of the Moon, the Eyrie looms large over the fertile lands of the Vale. Very few outsiders have ever attempted the dangerous journey skyward to its gates, except captured enemies sentenced to death within its walls. The infamous "sky cells" are known to drive prisoners to madness, who meet their doom via the Moon Door, which opens above a terrifying six-hundred-foot drop down the mountainside.

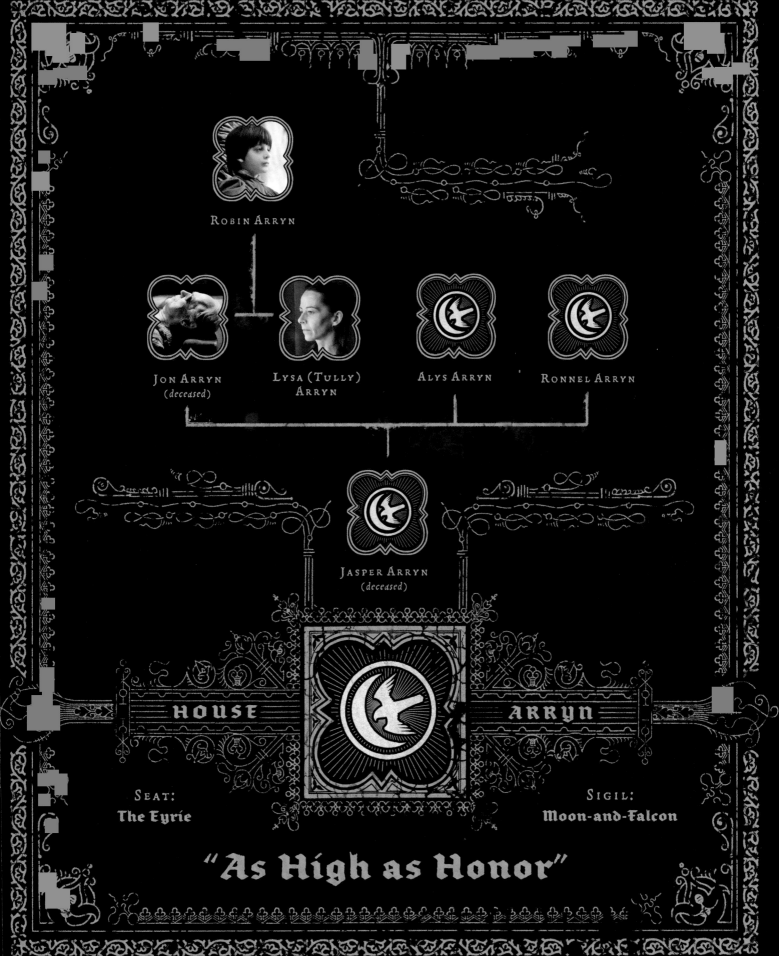

ROBIN ARRYN

JON ARRYN
(deceased)

LYSA (TULLY)
ARRYN

ALYS ARRYN

RONNEL ARRYN

JASPER ARRYN
(deceased)

HOUSE ARRYN

SEAT:
The Eyrie

SIGIL:
Moon-and-Falcon

"As High as Honor"

CREATING THE EYRIE

GEMMA JACKSON: **The book describes this amazing ascent up to the Eyrie. I just loved it, but unfortunately we couldn't do it for TV. That it was up above the clouds, it evolved in my mind as this kind of mad place. I'd been to Rome just before the first season started and visited the chapel at San Clemente. I decided to draw on those mosaics, to give the Eyrie a heavenly feel—not in any religious way, just using images of sky and birds. I love that set.**

DAVID BENIOFF: One my favorite sets from season one, the Eyrie shows off everything that makes Gemma Jackson and her department the best in the business. From the intricately tiled mosaic of birds in flight to the weirwood throne, the Eyrie is a gorgeous theater in the round. But what I love best about the room is that your eye is drawn to the falcon-and-moon bronze sigil covering a sliding door in the center of the floor. Falling through the Moon Door is the preferred manner of execution at the Eyrie. We've had one death by Moon Door so far—with more to come.

[above] *Tyrion is terrorized by the jailer Mord (Ciaran Bermingham) in the Eyrie sky cell.* ♦
[opposite] *The Eyrie exterior and High Hall, concept art.*

DANIEL MINAHAN (*director*): The premise for the Eyrie set was fantastic. And our production designer Gemma Jackson really went all out. That throne was remarkable—carved out of a huge gnarled piece of a tree that looked like it had been twisted by the

wind of the mountaintops. It was a utopian, beautiful space, in contrast to Lysa Arryn and the strange mountain people that inhabited the palace.

DAVID BENIOFF: While the nobles congregate in the Great Hall, condemned men languish in the sky cells, complete with sloping floors, ceilings, and only three walls, the better to show off the Eyrie's fantastic views of the Vale. Scrub away the blood graffiti on the walls, wash off the raw sewage running down the gutters, and you'd have a two-thousand-dollar-a-night luxury hotel room.

ADAM McINNES (*VFX supervisor, season one*): The view from the sky cell is one of the most "high-concept" visuals of the first season. Initial art department concepts, using the Huangshan mountains from China as a background, looked enticing,

but we needed somewhere closer to home that could be photographed. [Season one producer] Mark Huffam mentioned some mountains in Greece, and I found the Meteora mountain range, which even has a monastery perched unfeasibly way up on top, much like the Eyrie. Photographs of the mountains combined with matte painting created the environment we needed.

BRIAN KIRK *(director)*: The visual conceptualization of the different worlds, and the role of CGI in establishing them, was ongoing and constantly evolving, but there was room for fun, too. The sky cell, for example, was a simple moment of pure pleasure. Despite the existence of the storyboards, none of us during filming could have imagined how spectacular it would look. ❧

THE RIVERLANDS
A BRIEF HISTORY

The lands of the Trident River have been rife with conflict for centuries, due to their fertility and central location in Westeros. In the time of the First Men, many families vied to be Kings of the River and the Hills. The Mudd Kings were the last of the First Men to rise to power in the region.

[ABOVE] *Harrenhal concept art.*
❖ [RIGHT] *Arya and Gendry enter Harrenhal.* ❖ [OPPOSITE] *A section of the richly detailed Harrenhal set.*

Their last king, Tristifer the Fourth, valiantly fought against the Andal invaders, defeating them in ninety-nine separate engagements before finally succumbing. Centuries of fighting followed, with control of the region shifting between the Storm Kings and the ruthless warriors of the Iron Islands.

By the time Aegon Targaryen invaded Westeros, the lands of the Trident were decidedly part of the Iron Islands. King Harren the Black ruled over them, having just erected a colossal and monstrous stronghold, Harrenhal, as a symbol of his power.

Like many of the river lords, Edmyn Tully of Riverrun bore no love for the cruel King Harren. He supported Aegon's conquest of the region. When Aegon's dragons brought Harren to a fiery end (turning Harrenhal into a smoking ruin), the Tullys were made vassal lords to the crown and have governed the Riverlands ever since from their ancestral seat of Riverrun.

House Tully remained steadfast in support of the Targaryens until Robert Baratheon's rebellion some three hundred years later. Lord Hoster Tully's daughter, Catelyn, had been betrothed to Brandon Stark, the eldest son of the Warden of the North. When "Mad King" Aerys executed both Brandon and his father, Lord Hoster joined forces with Houses Stark, Arryn, and Baratheon against the crown. But his allegiance came with a price: Ned Stark married Catelyn in his brother's place, and Lord Jon Arryn of the Vale married Hoster's youngest daughter, Lysa. Lord Hoster proved a valuable ally on the battlefield, most notably aiding Robert in his victory at the Battle of the Bells. Today, House Tully of Riverrun remains a powerful and influential family in a volatile region, even as Lord Hoster is bedridden from illness and close to death.

GEMMA JACKSON (*production designer*): Harrenhal is supposed to be a huge, huge place, one that anyone should be proud to have, even though it's a total ruin. They sort of wave it around in the story, 'I'll give you Harrenhal!' It was important that it be impressive and unique. It was a tall order, as it's supposed to be one of the biggest castles in the story, one that was largely destroyed by dragonfire. We just went for it. We built a large court-yard space, with two levels and a bunch of corridors and smaller spaces within. It was designed in such a way that each space could represent different areas in the castle, depending on how you shot it—so it seems bigger than it actually is. Like Castle Black, it's meant to be one courtyard in a much larger castle, and CGI completes the picture.

DRAGONSTONE
A BRIEF HISTORY

Dragonstone is a small, rocky island in the Narrow Sea at the mouth of Blackwater Bay, near the capital city of King's Landing. This imposing citadel of volcanic rock was once the ancestral stronghold of House Targaryen.

When Robert Baratheon rebelled against the Iron Throne, "Mad King" Aerys sent his pregnant queen, Rhaella, and their youngest son, Prince Viserys, to Dragonstone for their safety. There, during a powerful thunderstorm that destroyed much of the Targaryen fleet, Daenerys Targaryen came into the world. She was ever after styled as "Daenerys Stormborn."

Yet Rhaella died in childbirth, and Viserys and Daenerys were spirited away by Targaryen loyalists across the Narrow Sea to the eastern continent of Essos. Dragonstone fell under Baratheon control, and King Robert gave the keep to his younger brother Stannis. Stannis bitterly resented this, as it meant the more valuable, prosperous, and well-manned keep of Storm's End was given to his younger brother, Renly.

Now, in the wake of King Robert's death, Stannis seeks to claim the Iron Throne, as he believes himself to be the true successor. He's aided in his quest by two loyal but decidedly different advisers: Davos Seaworth (Liam Cunningham), a common-born former smuggler knighted by Stannis, and the lady Melisandre (Carice van Houten), a mysterious and seductive red priestess from the far-eastern lands of Asshai.

[ABOVE] *Carice van Houten as Melisandre.* ❖ [OPPOSITE] *Liam Cunningham as Davos Seaworth.*

CREATING DRAGONSTONE

GEMMA JACKSON: Season two has a few locations that are more overtly "fantastical." With Dragonstone, the info in the book and script is pretty clear: it's a stronghold made up largely of dragon shapes carved out of volcanic rock. So what do you do? You carve a dragon out of volcanic rock! I did some research on Sigiriya, a massive rock-and-stone fortress in Sri Lanka, quite hair-raising, which has some amazing corridors carved in the rock. So we had that in mind as we designed our one Dragonstone set [Stannis Baratheon's map room].

The map room is one of my favorite sets in season two, a lovely challenge. It has some fun touches, like the vaguely Egyptian doors.

LIAM CUNNINGHAM (*Davos Seaworth*): The Dragonstone set is unbelievable. And the map table is gorgeous. It should be hanging on a wall somewhere—the Smithsonian!

GEMMA JACKSON: You really get an essence of the way maps were made in the old days, where the perspective is a bit off. George's book describes it as something like fifty feet long! We obviously couldn't do that, but I love what we came up with. ❧

TINA JONES: My biggest contribution [to the Dragonstone set] was Stannis's map table. I kept thinking of those World War II maps, like the ones found in Churchill's map rooms, and the idea of highlighting the most important areas of the continent. We came up with the idea of precious stones and metals to indicate forests and strongholds—bits of bone for the castle, emeralds for the trees, molten copper for the roads—the idea being the map's landmarks could easily be seen in this dark space. [Supervising prop maker] Gavin Jones did an amazing job building it.

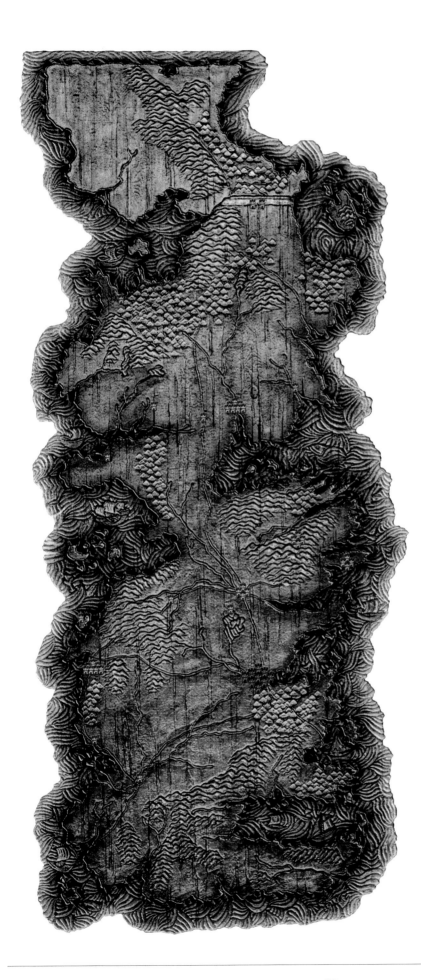

[opposite top and above] *Dragonstone, early exterior concept art.* ♦ [opposite bottom] *Dragonstone, interior concept art.* ♦ [left] *Map table concept art.*

Stannis Baratheon

The younger brother of Robert Baratheon, Stannis believes himself to be Robert's true heir and has declared himself king but has difficulty getting widespread support for his claim. Cold, decisive, and lacking in warmth, Stannis does possess a strict moral code, which is tested as he is forced to wage war against his own family.

VANESSA TAYLOR *(executive producer, writer, season two):* One of my favorite characters in season two, Stannis Baratheon [played by Stephen Dillane], has lived his life trying to play by the rules, do everything right, make the sacrifices it takes to engage in righteous behavior—and nobody cares. They'd rather have someone charismatic. It's the dilemma faced by anyone who's ever been the good, homework-doing, rule-abiding kid wondering why some big goof-off is popularity king. His claim to the throne is legitimate, but no one gives him the time of day. To me he has a kind of quiet dignity and yet is not particularly likable. Stephen Dillane gets all this and also brings to the part a certain enigmatic depth that makes me want to see what he does going forward.

[ABOVE AND OPPOSITE] *Stephen Dillane as Stannis Baratheon.*

MELISANDRE

Melisandre is an influential counselor of Stannis Baratheon and a red priestess from Asshai, a mysterious region in the far east. She is possessed of prophetic powers and capable of dark magic. Beautiful, highly sensual, and seductive, she is also extremely dangerous to any who dare stand in her way.

VANESSA TAYLOR: Melisandre [played by Carice Van Houten] is important because she's one of the characters that takes us into the realm of fantasy in an active way. So much of the story feels more real, more grounded, but Melisandre is a mystic, gifted with magical powers. As such, the casting of this part was crucial, and Carice has to straddle that line of being both fantastical and grounded; otherworldly and real all at once.

DAVOS SEAWORTH

Once a lowborn and infamous smuggler, Davos Seaworth became a knight in Stannis Baratheon's service after deeds of heroism during Robert's rebellion. While he has never forgotten his roots, he is devoted to Stannis and is considered his most honest and trusted adviser; he is wary of the war his master is about to wage.

LIAM CUNNINGHAM: Davos is a tricky character. He's a man of few words, mainly because, in the book, it's almost all POV stuff, inside his head. What I love about him is his unwavering loyalty to a difficult man [Stannis Baratheon]. That kind of paradox—Davos comes in and saves the day and his initial reward is getting his fingers chopped off! I love the irony of that. Stannis has this speech, "The good doesn't wash out the bad nor the bad the good." I think Davos has an enormous respect for that, and he's duly rewarded, being put in this consigliere position. I said this to Stephen Dillane when we were rehearsing: Davos is sort of a Jiminy Cricket to this guy—his conscience. He's a good man. He tries to do the right thing. But he's tested by Melisandre, who has just come on the scene. So much of season two is this great push and pull between the two of them, with Stannis in the middle. It's great stuff to play. A lot of it is in the pauses, the looks, the silences.

[OPPOSITE] *Carice van Houten as Melisandre.* ❖ [BELOW] *Liam Cunningham as Davos Seaworth.*

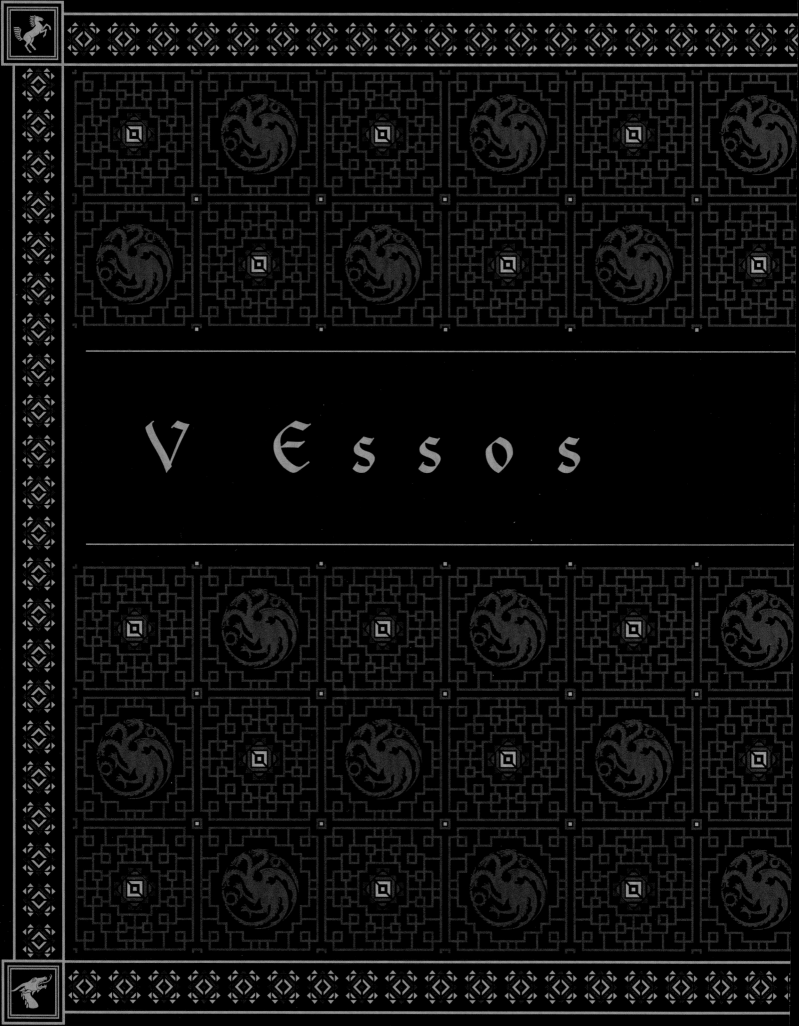

V Essos

{ House Targaryen }

ESSOS

A BRIEF HISTORY

> "It won't be long now. Soon you will cross the
> Narrow Sea and take back your father's throne."
>
> —Magister Illyrio to Viserys Targaryen

East of Westeros, across the Narrow Sea, is the great continent of Essos. A huge landmass of varying climate, geography, and cultures, the continent currently has no single ruler. Instead, the western areas of Essos are home to the nine Free Cities, which include Lys, Volantis, Braavos, and the major port city of Pentos.

All (save Braavos) were once colonies of the extinct Valyrian empire but now operate as independent city-states. The Free Cities are active trading partners with the Seven Kingdoms of Westeros, due to their proximity.

Further east, the sweeping grasslands of the Dothraki Sea stretch for miles and miles. Largely unsettled, they are lorded over by the Dothraki, a nomadic culture of fearsome horselords, who prowl the continent in hordes known as *khalasars*. The most feared and renowned Dothraki warrior, Khal Drogo, was betrothed to Daenerys Targaryen in the hopes that he might lead an army of Dothraki to take back the Seven Kingdoms. The Dothraki capitol, Vaes Dothrak, is home to their sacred temple and is their only permanent settlement.

South of the Dothraki Sea are the hilly lands of Lhazar. Its inhabitants, the Lhazareen, are a simple culture of shepherds, known throughout the conti-

nent as "Lamb Men." They are frequent victims of Dothraki raids. Beyond Lhazar, farther east, is the Red Waste, an inhospitable, arid desert not even the bravest Dothraki horde dares enter.

On the far eastern side of the Red Waste, on the shores of the Jade Sea, lies the ancient city of Qarth. The center of the east, the port city teems with galleys from every corner of the world, including the eastern lands of Asshai and Yi Ti. The city is renowned for its wealth, sophisticated culture, opulence, and unparalleled beauty. It is governed by the Thirteen, an esteemed organization of powerful merchants, many of whom pride themselves as "pureborn" descendants of Qarth's ancient kings and queens. It is also home to the Warlocks, mysterious beings who practice dark magic in a shadowy ruin called the House of the Undying. However, their power has waned over the centuries, and with it, their prestige.

[ABOVE] *Khal Drogo (Jason Momoa) and his Bloodriders.* ❖ [OPPOSITE] *A Dothraki totem.*

CREATING ESSOS

DAVID BENIOFF (executive producer, writer):
Essos is so vast, so mysterious, so diverse that we needed *three* separate countries to capture it. At various times, we've shot in Morocco, Malta, and Croatia. Make that four countries, since we shot the Dothraki Sea in Northern Ireland, in a willow field grown to our specifications.

IAIN GLEN (Jorah Mormont):
It makes me giggle that our story line is almost entirely played out in the most exotic of locations.

As the other actors freeze their rocks off at Castle Black and Winterfell, our nomadic journey takes us from one slice of paradise to another. I keep joking with the producers that although nearly everything Daenerys and Jorah do in their story is informed by the objective of returning to their birthplace, I kind of hope they don't get there too quickly!

THE DOTHRAKI SEA & VAES DOTHRAK

GEMMA JACKSON (production designer):
For Vaes Dothrak, the city of the Horselords, I did quite a bit of research on the Pacific Islands and on indigenous people

using materials to build shelters. I spent time in Vanuatu, where there are these structures built without using nails—with bent, curved fronts. Everything is woven and light. So the structures in Vaes Dothrak grew from there. [Concept artist] Ashleigh Jeffers interpreted these ideas in his concept drawings, and we built them on the soundstage in Belfast. We also drew some inspiration from African imagery, particularly for the Temple of the Dosh Khaleen.

DAVID BENIOFF:
The temple set was a favorite of mine from season one. It featured these totem pole–type objects

[top] *Filming the Dothraki camp, with Northern Ireland doubling for Essos.* ♦ [left] *Ser Jorah (Iain Glen), Daenerys (Emilia Clarke), and the Dothraki* khalasar. ♦ [opposite] *Viserys Targaryen (Harry Lloyd) looks out over the Dothraki Sea.*

boasting horse heads and giant phalluses. I wanted to take one home, but my wife said no.

MICHELE CLAPTON (*costume designer*): The look for the Dothraki changed a bit between the original pilot and the filming of the series, and it was a tricky one to get. There was danger of going too far in one direction, too far into strictly African or Native American. Originally, their look was a bit more theatrical, but we brought it down by taking it straight back to their environment. What do they have access to? Well, there's grass from the grasslands; the women weave. And there are skins from small animals.

All the colors were quite natural and one with the land, but we wanted to give it something else. So we developed this blue paint, this pigment, that maybe they developed by crushing stones, and that they used relatively sparingly for celebrations—like the wedding in Episode 101. Visually it became much more exciting, this blue within this very barren landscape.

We also looked at a lot of images of Afghani horsemen, which inspired the Dothraki riding boots. We imagined their footwear would be designed to accommodate riding first and foremost, since they're a horse culture. So they have these heels that keep their feet in the stirrups. And, if you're riding, you need trousers—leather trousers—even Daenerys had them under her skirts, as do some of the other Dothraki women. But we didn't want to be frivolous about it—the weaving was practical and gave it a nice texture. ❧

HOUSE TARGARYEN

A BRIEF HISTORY

"You don't want to wake the dragon, do you?"

—Viserys Targaryen

The Targaryens are "Blood of the Dragon," descended from Old Valyria, a once-mighty kingdom that ruled Essos for five thousand years. Their true origins have been lost to time, but the first Valyrians were allegedly a community of shepherds, tending their flocks on a small peninsula on Essos. That changed forever when they made a shocking discovery. Within a volcanic area known as the Fourteen Fires, they discovered monstrous, scaled creatures with sharp claws, massive wings, and fiery breath—dragons.

In time, the Valyrians tamed the dragons and discovered their deep-rooted connection to magic. Harnessing the beasts' incredible power, they established a city of uncommon wonder, unlike any before or since. They also became skilled at sorcery and metallurgy, creating weapons of spell-forged steel. Wielding these weapons astride their dragons, the Valyrians conquered the surrounding lands and expanded west.

At the time, much of Essos was dominated by the Ghiscari Empire. The Ghiscari legions tried to stop the Valyrian expansion, but to no avail; they attacked the Valyrians five times and were each time defeated. Finally, the Valyrians marched on their capitol, Old Ghis, and obliterated it, turning its streets and buildings to ash with dragonflame. Today, the last remnants of Ghiscari civilization can be found in the city-states of Slaver's Bay.

In contrast, the Freehold of Valyria became the most advanced civilization in the known world—with its own language, gods, and culture—and its great cities and paved roads extended over the continent. The Freehold prospered for eons and then came the cataclysmic event known only as "The Doom," a mysterious devastation that destroyed Old Valyria. The peninsula itself was shattered, becoming what is now the Smoking Sea, which most sailors consider demon-haunted. Every dragon was lost—or so it was believed—along with the Valyrians' spells, knowledge, and recorded history. Their mighty empire collapsed, and one by one, Valyria's western colonies declared their independence.

But House Targaryen survived, having settled on the distant island fortress of Dragonstone years before. They remained there for a century, until the rise of Aegon the Conqueror.

In accordance with Valyrian custom, Aegon took both of his sisters, Visenya and Rhaenys, as his wives, keeping the bloodlines pure. His sister-wives at his side, he sailed west for the Seven Kingdoms, determined to create an empire even greater than that of his ancestors. Aegon's host was greatly outnumbered, but he possessed a unique weapon: the last of the dragons. Each beast was named for the Valyrian gods of Aegon's forefathers. Visenya rode Vhaghar, Rhaenys rode Meraxes, and Aegon rode Balerion the Black Dread—with fire dark as night and wings so huge whole towns were covered in shadow when he flew overhead. Aegon and his sisters conquered every kingdom save Dorne, which would eventually submit to Targaryen rule more than a century later.

The line of Dragon Kings was finally broken when Aerys the Second, known as the "Mad King," was overthrown in rebellion and killed by Ser Jaime Lannister, a member of Aerys's own Kingsguard. Aerys's son and heir, Prince Rhaegar, perished on the field of battle at the hands of Robert Baratheon, who claimed the Iron Throne for himself. And so, today, the only surviving members of the Targaryen dynasty are Prince Viserys and his sister, Daenerys, who were spirited away to the Free Cities of Essos by loyalists. They have lived in exile ever since.

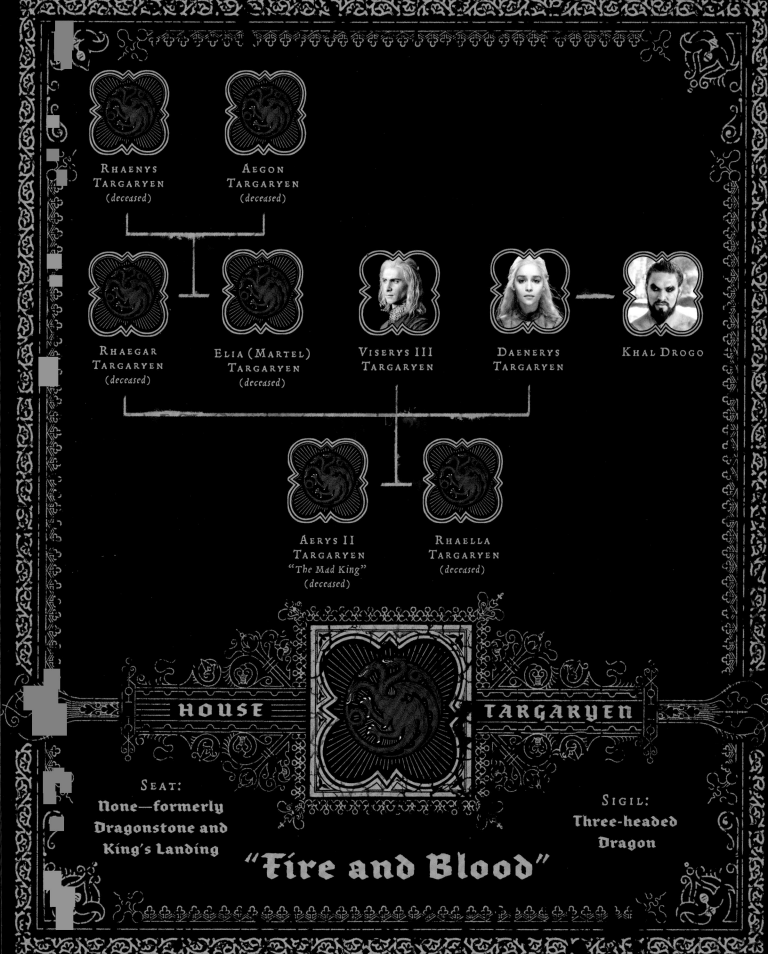

RHAENYS
TARGARYEN
(deceased)

AEGON
TARGARYEN
(deceased)

RHAEGAR
TARGARYEN
(deceased)

ELIA (MARTEL)
TARGARYEN
(deceased)

VISERYS III
TARGARYEN

DAENERYS
TARGARYEN

KHAL DROGO

AERYS II
TARGARYEN
"The Mad King"
(deceased)

RHAELLA
TARGARYEN
(deceased)

HOUSE   TARGARYEN

SEAT:
None—formerly
Dragonstone and
King's Landing

SIGIL:
Three-headed
Dragon

"Fire and Blood"

Daenerys Targaryen

An exiled princess and the last of the overthrown Targaryen line, Daenerys spent her entire life far from Westeros, in hiding on the eastern continent of Essos. Timid and innocent at first, she grows into a steely and strong leader after her marriage to the Dothraki horse-lord Khal Drogo, the death of her domineering brother Viserys, and the birth of her dragons—the first in thousands of years. Her mission: reclaim her family's birthright and take back the Iron Throne.

DANIEL MINAHAN (*director, season one*): I love all the characters, but I think my favorite is Daenerys. Her journey is so archetypal—how she's sold into slavery and turns it around and becomes a queen, determined to take back the throne for her family. She's only a girl, so it's interesting to watch how she moves through the world, makes mistakes, and learns really hard lessons because of her own ambition.

D. B. WEISS: To be a young actress and make the journey from frightened young girl to a fantasy Joan of Arc—it wasn't like you could look for someone who had "done this sort of thing before." There are plenty of opportunities for young women to be scared, abused, and terrorized in film and television, but there are virtually no roles that let them step into the fire—literally or otherwise—and come out the other side reborn as a leader and a warrior with an otherworldly poise and strength. So much was riding on the ability of the actress who played Dany to do just this. For a long time, it seemed like this might be a serious, perhaps insurmountable problem.

DAVID BENIOFF: Our wonderful casting director, Nina Gold, brought Emilia Clarke in to read for the part—I believe Emilia had graduated from drama school a few weeks earlier. Her résumé consisted of a public service commercial and a guest appearance on a British soap I'd never heard of before. Not the CV you're looking for when casting Daenerys Targaryen, First of Her Name.

D. B. WEISS: Then we saw Emilia's first audition on a two-inch laptop window in David's kitchen. She was doing the preamble to her "step into the fire" from Episode 110,

money. She works harder than anyone, but she also has a very rare gift, and it didn't take more than a few seconds to see it.

In her final audition for HBO, when she flew out to do what must have been a mortifying command performance in front of all of us and several HBO executives, she nailed it. And then she did the Robot. I'm not sure she nailed the Robot, but she committed to it 100 percent, and five minutes later she had the job. It's impossible to imagine anyone else in the role, and impossible to imagine the show without her.

DAVID BENIOFF: Emilia didn't just win the part. She owned the part. She owned the early-season Dany material, when the young exile is timid and nearly silent, living in her abusive brother's shadow. And she owned the later-season

and it was like being shot from the screen with a laser beam. Or a tractor beam. Definitely some kind of beam. She came to it fully formed; every instinct and inflection was right on the

EMILIA CLARKE: When I first read the script, it was the first time as a young actress that I'd found a character that's so multidimensional. You're often pigeonholed—she's either a shrew or an innocent. But with Dany, you've got it all. You have a real human being who is scared but manages to overcome it. I just clicked with her. I can't really explain it. She's real to me. I empathize with her. I believe in her.

material, when Daenerys Stormborn, *khaleesi* of the Dothraki, becomes a true queen.

HARRY LLOYD (*Viserys Targaryen*): Emilia did become like a sister to me, very quickly. When you have to be completely horrible to someone on-screen, it helps to have a good relationship offscreen. And we're geeks, truthfully. We wanted to find out everything we could about the Targaryen family history, so we reread the books together.

EMILIA CLARKE: I feel very lucky to have the books, more than anything. It's a huge treat for me, as an actor, to have her thoughts written down, or at least a kind of guide to her thoughts. It really helped me get into her in season one, to be able to refer back to it. It's as if it went from George's mind into the book, into my mind, then out my mouth.

I take a lot of pride in my work and in what I do. If I'm going to do something, I want to do it right. I try to put as much work and love and care into it as I can. But this had an extra level to it, and I don't think I quite realized the enormity of this show until later. Had I realized just how big it was early on, I might have just collapsed in fear. I think that I knew, but my brain just programmed itself to focus on it like anything else I'd do.

I went to drama school, but I needn't have—*Game of Thrones* has been the biggest lesson on acting you could ever have. It's such a special thing to be a part of, and I really feel that. Even if I had done a lot of stuff before this, it would still be special. I struck lucky that it was my first big job!

[ABOVE] *Former concubine Doreah teaches Dany the art of seduction.* ❖ [BELOW] *Special maquettes of Dany's three dragons were used during the filming of season two.* ❖ [OPPOSITE] *Dany examines her wedding present: three dragon eggs, which the ages have turned to stone.*

COSTUMING DANY

MICHELE CLAPTON: At the start of the series, Dany has lived most her life being told how to dress, initially by her brother. She has two key dresses in the first episode: her "viewing" dress and her wedding dress. The "viewing" dress is essentially designed to make her look naked, as Drogo's come to see the goods, basically. It's accented by these dragon-head brooches, which also hold it up. As for the wedding dress, it was meant to unwrap, as if Drogo is opening a present. And, of course, at the end of the first season, she burns in it, which is rather poignant—the end of her story with Drogo.

Dany steps into Dothraki society and grows within it. Her costume throughout

[above] *Dany's evolving look in season two, blending Dothraki and Qartheen styles.* ◆
[opposite top] *Dany's "viewing" dress, worn at her first meeting with Khal Drogo.* ◆
[opposite middle] *Costume concept for the metal corset Dany wears in Qarth.* ◆ [opposite bottom] *Dany as* khaleesi *with a scaly dragon-esque top.* ◆ [opposite right] *Dany's wedding dress, trimmed with dragon-head brooches.*

the season reflects that. She starts off with a basic Dothraki outfit, but as she evolves, she ends up having a bit more ornamenta-tion. When she goes to the market in Vaes Dothrak, she buys what looks like a dragon-skin top and starts to create her own look, within the Dothraki style.

Dany takes what's presented to her, adapts it, and evolves with it. In season two, she arrives in Qarth, completely broken, and she is initially won over by the Qartheen style—this beautiful, reveal-ing, turquoise dress . . . but then realizes it's not quite right. It's not her. So she starts wearing this gold corset over her Dothraki costume, then eventually a leather corset over a Qartheen man's top, blending the two cultures and creating her own style. ❧

Viserys Targaryen

*"Who can rule
without wealth or fear or love?"*
—Viserys Targaryen

A deposed prince living in exile on Essos with his younger sister, Daenerys, Viserys is known as "the Beggar King," having spent his entire life in hiding, begging for money and shelter while scheming for a way to reclaim the Iron Throne for himself. Hot-tempered and prone to fits of anger, Viserys is cruel and abusive to Daenerys, marrying her off to the Dothraki horselord Khal Drogo in exchange for an army that could take back the Seven Kingdoms.

GEORGE R. R. MARTIN (*executive producer, author*): The most prominent inspiration [for the exiled Targaryens] were the Stuarts, who were driven from the English throne. The "King Across the Water," Bonnie Prince Charlie, periodically invaded England and was always failing. Three generations of Stuarts tried to take back the throne. Of course, if they had dragons, it might have turned out differently!

the time. He doesn't see himself as a villain. He's the hero of this story! That's how you have to play it: "I'm the fucking lead! Why isn't anyone treating me like the lead?"

MICHELE CLAPTON: Regarding the family sigils, we generally wanted to avoid having characters wearing them on their chests, like Superman or something, but Viserys is the one character that sports this huge [dragon] sigil doublet. He wears it the whole time, as if to scream, "I'm a Targaryen!" And it gets more battered and dirtied as the season goes on and he gets further and further away from what he wants. It's a lovely way to reflect this blind hope; the costume fades with him.

EMILIA CLARKE: It's an insane dynamic between Dany and her brother. Viserys is the only family Dany has ever had. Every single thing Dany knows has come from her brother—everything. I had to try to imagine what it must feel like to have so many natural, instinctive thought processes shot down again and again. And she's grown up her whole life thinking she's going to *marry* him.

HARRY LLOYD: In the book, you never get to see inside his mind. You only see him through Dany, who doesn't understand his motives, so he appears the villain. As an actor, I had to see the story, and his role in it, through his point of view. Otherwise, he would just be sneering and screaming all

HARRY LLOYD: His is a singular obsession that drives everything: he want his family's throne back, his birthright. It's like a religion, something he never questioned. So you can't wink. You have to take it extremely seriously.

[OPPOSITE] *Harry Lloyd as Viserys Targaryen.*

THE CROWNING OF VISERYS

EPISODE 106: "A GOLDEN CROWN"

THERE WERE QUITE A FEW "GAME-CHANGER" SEQUENCES IN SEASON ONE, AND "THE CROWNING OF VISERYS" PROVED TO BE ONE OF THE MOST INFAMOUS AND MEMORABLE. PULLING OFF SUCH A TECHNICALLY COMPLICATED AND EMOTIONALLY POWERFUL SCENE ON SCHEDULE AND ON BUDGET PROVED TO BE A HIGH-WIRE ACT FOR THE CAST AND CREW.

DANIEL MINAHAN: I was shocked when I first read the scene, not so much that Viserys was getting killed off—I figured he had it coming—but the way it was done. I'd never read anything quite like it, and I didn't know how we would do it. It's a pretty tall order, when you think about it: melt down a belt, pour molten gold over a guy's head, and watch him burn to death.

HARRY LLOYD: Viserys has been liberated by the alcohol; he's free. And he turns up at this party with a secret—"I know just what to do here, and I'm not scared of any of you people." It turns from the best day of his life, really, to the last day of his life.

DANIEL MINAHAN: I was sad to see Viserys go. He was a worthy villain, and Harry Lloyd and I really wanted to give him his due. In rehearsals, we kept coming back to the idea that Viserys had this childlike quality about him. He was a kid who had the responsibility of the honor of his family on his shoulders, and I'm not sure he really understood what he was doing in that final scene, when he pulls that sword and threatens Dany's unborn baby. He's a tragic character.

This scene required that every single department come together to pull it off. It took an elaborate rig of smoke machines, multiples of costumes and wigs, and the special effects involved in pouring molten gold over Viserys's head. First, finding the right consistency of gold liquid that the

"He was no dragon. Fire cannot kill a dragon."

{ Daenerys Targaryen }

———※———

special effects people could get to bubble without actually being hot, then hiding all the machines on Harry's body that would create the steam, then a temporary less-expensive wig for Harry that we could destroy, an alternate burned costume, a prosthetic helmet for him to wear in the last shot, burn makeup, and so on.

It was going to be very involved and time-consuming, so we called all the departments together for a test in the Paint Hall,

a few days before the shoot. We had an assistant from the Special Effects department—wearing a long white fright wig—as our test subject. He gave a halfhearted scream and flailed his arms around a little and finally pretended to die, which broke everyone down into peals of laughter. The gold looked great, but the smoke was too much and too white. But with some minor adjustments, this could just work!

The day finally came and we realized we had only one shot at this because of our limited schedule. There was simply too much reset time for wigs and makeup to do a second take or even get another angle. Harry remained cool as a cucumber. But I could tell Jason Momoa was actually a bit nervous, which is completely out of character for him. There was a lot of pressure on him, as he had to take this thing of molten gold, hit his target, and play the scene, all in one take.

EMILIA CLARKE: My friendship with Harry made it possible for me to tap into the real struggle Dany has with Viserys, in that he's her brother and she loves him. So when that amazing moment happens, when he's threatening her child—it takes something like that for her to really turn against him. That's an animalistic, maternal thing; when you've got a connection to your child, everything else goes out the window. But even then, after everything, she speaks of him with sorrow, not anger or bitterness. Harry made that possible for me.

HARRY LLOYD: When we shot that moment after Dany tells me Drogo's going to give me a crown, I couldn't help but play the awkwardness of the situation. He kind of giggles there, almost as if he's embarrassed. I imagine in that moment he's looking at Drogo as if to say, "Okay, what now? I'm going to get my crown. So let's talk . . . army? Or should we leave that for tomorrow?" Then somebody comes up and breaks Viserys's arm. Even then he probably assumes it's a translation issue! It's only when Drogo goes for the pot that he stops saying, "I am the dragon," and starts pleading for his life.

DANIEL MINAHAN: We had two cameras. One was behind Harry looking at Jason—placed so we couldn't see the smoke rigs on Harry—and the other was on Harry's face. I'm pretty sure everyone in the company came to the Paint Hall that day to see it happen. And we got it! I think it came off really well. The VFX team did a few enhancements in postproduction, but for the most part, what you see on-screen is all practical. Harry really sold the idea of this person being burned to death.

HARRY LLOYD: As I remember it, there was the initial shock of the pain, and then there was this high-pitched girlie scream. It's almost as if he's dead already — the same way you see corpses twitching. That's not the sound of someone who's alive. I just let it all go, took a deep breath, and screamed as long as I could.

JASON MOMOA (Khal Drogo): Man, I loved that scene. Drogo enjoys the violence. He gets this sadistic pleasure from it. I remember all of us crowding around the monitors to watch the playback of that shot where the molten gold hits his head. It was sick!

DANIEL MINAHAN: We had this shot, with the camera on the ground, where we see his face hit the ground, with the prosthetic "golden crown" and all this horrible burn makeup. Poor Harry had to fall and smack the floor about ten times before we got it just right.

HARRY LLOYD: You know what was my favorite bit in the end? When they put in the sound effect you hear when my golden head smacks the floor. I was at home with some mates, watching it for the first time, and when that moment came—CLANK—we screamed! It's a big turning point in the series, I think, in that it's the first major death in terms of main characters. Of course, people start dropping like flies from that moment on.

D. B. WEISS: This scene was nominated for a Spike TV Scream Award for "Most Memorable Mutilation." It lost to Piranha 3D. In my objective opinion, the voting body for the Scream Awards made a huge mistake here. Harry Lloyd played this scene with so many layers and facets—the recklessness that comes from complete hopelessness, the unhinged abandon, his childlike joy when he thinks for a brief moment that he's finally getting the only thing he ever wanted. Add to this Drogo's Eastwood-y relish in Viserys's demise, the stone-cold delivery of Dany's finishing line, Dan Minahan's artful direction, Matt Jensen's great photography: I could not be happier with the way this one came together. ॐ

JORAH MORMONT

A disgraced knight, Ser Jorah has been exiled from Westeros for several years. He throws in with the deposed prince Viserys but soon becomes a devoted follower to his sister Daenerys. Jorah is a strong and capable warrior with vast knowledge of the varied regions and cultures of Essos. He is an indispensable ally to Dany but is haunted by a troubled past and a terrible secret: He once informed on Dany to King Robert, resulting in an assassination attempt that nearly took her life.

IAIN GLEN: I could see from the outline that if I was going to play Jorah, I would be in it for the long haul. His journey is a slow burn through the course of many seasons. Such roles afford the opportunity to develop character more roundly—more like real life, I guess, where personality reveals itself over time as situations and relationships change. It felt like a luxury not to have to show too much too quickly.

DAVID BENIOFF: In George's novels, Jorah Mormont is a bald brute. Iain Glen, on the other hand, is a handsome Scottish gentleman of surpassing charm and grace. We worried about this role quite a bit before we shot the pilot. Since Jorah has traveled extensively in Essos and Dany has not, he serves as her tour guide, constantly explaining locales and Dothraki customs. We didn't want him to become Jorah the Explorer. Luckily, as William Goldman would say, the problem was solved in casting. Iain could read the legalese in an iTunes licensing agreement and somehow make it compelling. He possesses that rare combination of a leading man's presence and a character actor's subtle brilliance. We are very lucky to have him.

EMILIA CLARKE: Iain really takes care of me, and he did from day one. I think he saw an inexperienced young actress who wanted to do the right thing, and he guided me in a really great way.

"**Does loyalty mean nothing to you?**"
—Viserys Targaryen

"**It means everything to me.**"
—Jorah Mormont

IAIN GLEN: It appealed to me that Jorah develops [from a spy] into a companion who has a clear and pure intent. *Game of Thrones* portrays a dark world of warring, hostile, and fractious dynasties, where leaders will stop at nothing to promote their claims. Within this cruel and unforgiving landscape it felt a valuable contrast to witness a good and honest soldier commit himself to the welfare of his queen. Deep down, Ser Jorah is a kind soul, and there is a tenderness that distinguishes his and Dany's relationship.

EMILIA CLARKE: Dany's desperately searching for a father figure, and with Jorah, she instantly finds that. For her, it's a paternal thing going on. Of course, as she becomes more aware of life and of men in general, she realizes that he's not her father, and there's something else going on there.

IAIN GLEN: The crucial complication is that Jorah falls passionately in love with Dany. He shows admirable restraint in hiding his love, probably because his instinct tells him she won't return the love and he fears rejection. As long as he can nurse his secret love, it remains a beguiling possibility. Jorah possesses a romantic heart, and his life has been repeatedly blighted by unrequited love. It seems to be part of who he is. The strength and nature of his feelings will eventually spill out of him and taint their relationship forever.

[ABOVE AND OPPOSITE] *Iain Glen as Ser Jorah Mormont.*

:Khal Drogo

"Khal Drogo has never been defeated.
He's a savage, of course, but one of the finest killers alive.
And you will be his queen."

—Viserys Targaryen

Khal Drogo is a powerful warlord of the Dothraki, a nomadic, tribal nation of riders who raid and pillage across Essos. A mighty warrior who has never been defeated in battle, he is both loved and feared by his followers, who are known as his khalasar. In return for the promise of an army, exiled prince Viserys Targaryen offers Drogo the hand of his sister, Daenerys, in marriage. Their captor-captive relationship eventually changes into one of real love.

JASON MOMOA (Khal Drogo): Reading the audition sides, the thing that got me was how raw and powerful it was; you don't see that kind of thing on TV. Drogo just came screaming off the page. There was something, on a primal level, that was so raw about him. Of course, he has this rage, but there's also something in him that's so in tune with the earth and his culture and himself. I've never had a character speak to me that way on a first read. I went out and got the first book, so I could better understand what was going on, and I was hooked immediately. I mean, I'd never read that big a book, or that particular genre of book, so fast. I was out of commission for three days. I just locked myself up and read.

A lot of people when they watch the first few episodes are like, "Well, he doesn't do much. You just sit there with your shirt off, Momoa, good job." But just wait, man. . . . Drogo sneaks up on the audience. I was looking at footage of silverback gorillas, and a silverback can just stare at you, and you know if you're in trouble. You can feel the temperature in the air change. I wanted him to have that quality, that stillness, in those first few episodes, so that when he has those explosive moments later on, it's a big deal.

D. B. WEISS: Jason's Dothraki monologue in Episode 107 was one of the high points of the first season. Extras aren't always the most enthusiastic bunch, but he got them so riled up they were ready to go kill someone, even though they didn't have the slightest idea what he was saying.

JASON MOMOA: You know when Drogo would get amped up? I did all this research on the Apaches Geronimo and Cochise, and also Genghis Khan, and funnily enough, Hitler! I remember seeing *Triumph of the Will*—he was crazy when he delivered those speeches, the physicality, the way he spat out the words and rallied all those people. So, I ended up using some of that in the big scene where Drogo riles up his men.

EMILIA CLARKE: Jason . . . I don't think I'm ever going to meet anyone else like Jason. It was a crazy adventure with him; he was a joy to work with. My favorite moment is when he's riling up the *khalasar*, and I'm looking at him with such love: "That's my man. He's gonna kill for me." It's such a huge, intense moment, and it enabled the stuff we did in the final episodes of the season.

JASON MOMOA: Those final scenes [in Episode 110], staring out into the sun, were very hard. I had to meditate and slow myself down for a while. I would practice all these faces at home, with my wife, trying to figure out what his face would look like in that kind of catatonic state. She was laughing at me! I figured it would be like what happens to your face after you have a stroke, so I sucked my jaw back a little and did this thing with my eyes where they were slightly crossed. It was important for me to show how this indestructible guy could waste away.

D. B. WEISS: Jason's charisma and talent are matched only by his decency, thoughtfulness, and freakish physical strength. Drogo could so easily have been a cartoon. The dimension, thoughtfulness, and instincts that Jason brought were a godsend. When he'd say, "Drogo would say or do this, or Drogo wouldn't say or do that," he was right every time.

JASON MOMOA: Hey, look, to me, Drogo's the nicest guy in the whole thing. Everyone else is all conniving and shit, but he wears his heart on his sleeve. You know where you stand with him. I think he's a good man. He's just from a different world. There's a purity about him.

[ABOVE] *Drogo does battle with an insolent Dothraki warrior.* ❖ [OPPOSITE] *Drogo holding court at the (recently sacked) temple of the Lhazareen.* ❖ [PREVIOUS SPREAD] *Jason Momoa as Khal Drogo.*

DANIEL MINAHAN: I think the love story between Dany and Khal Drogo is amazing, and they were an incredible team. Emilia and Jason created this deep bond between their characters. And let's face it, they were hot together.

EMILIA CLARKE: It was a really organic process, figuring out the evolution of their relationship. You start with the wedding night. As an actor, I looked at it this way: if that were me, that's a rape. It's horrific and horrible, and no matter what Dany's been through with Viserys, nothing has prepared her for that. I think that she, for the first time, realizes that it's sink or swim. I don't think there are many people who would take control of that kind of situation the way she does and declare that she's not going to be a victim.

JASON MOMOA: Emilia's like my little sister, so it was really tough working on those scenes. They were really intense and painful, and I was constantly trying to make sure she was okay. We did a lot of drinking afterward.

EMILIA CLARKE: For me, the change actually happened in the scene as we were shooting it—it's the scene [in Episode 102] that occurs after Doreah has kindly showed me a few techniques for the bedroom. I remember it really well, as it turned out to be the final scene we shot for season one. The scene needed to go from victim to woman taking control to a real love scene, and I didn't know if we were going to pull that off. But something in Jason's eyes just went, as if he woke up for the first time: "I don't have to do this thing that I've been taught my entire life." Suddenly they saw each other for the first time, and it blossomed from there. I don't think Dany is prepared for that happening.

I think if it had been anyone else, he would have smacked her down and continued to rape her. But there's something about Drogo that was better, that Dany had to draw out. Maybe it was a blessing that scene kept getting pushed back in the schedule until, finally, it was the last day and we had to shoot it! Maybe we needed to have lived with the characters all those months in order to find that moment.

JASON MOMOA: There's a moment where love just comes in. Drogo's infatuated and attracted to how different she is, but then there is a moment where it clicks—where he looks into her soul and it becomes love. He suddenly becomes vulnerable. In the end, the man is still a human being and he can see beauty.

CREATING THE DOTHRAKI LANGUAGE

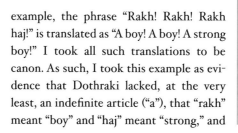

DAVID BENIOFF: The Dothraki are an alien people to Dany, and she finds herself trying desperately to understand them. So we wanted to feel her distance from her new tribe—to hear their language and comprehend just as little as Dany does.

D.B. WEISS: If we were ever going to feel what it was like to be in her situation, we needed the sense of disorientation that comes with not understanding a word anyone around you is saying.

DAVID BENIOFF: But we're not linguists. If we had attempted to invent the language ourselves, it would have been ridiculous "ooga booga" stuff. So we went to an expert. David Peterson's Dothraki is a thing of beauty, a language that sounds absolutely real and lived-in even though it didn't exist a couple of years ago.

JASON MOMOA: The audition scene was in broken English, as it is in the books. But when I showed up on the first day, David and Dan said, "Well, it doesn't make much sense for this whole tribe to learn English. It's more likely Dany would learn Dothraki." That made sense. Then they told me, "So you're going to be speaking *all of your dialogue* in Dothraki." And I thought, "Uh-oh. What?" It turned out to be such an amazing, beautiful language.

DAVID J. PETERSON *(linguist)*: The very first thing I did in creating the language was record every Dothraki name, word,

and phrase from George's books. In the end, I had a list that comprised about thirty words, most of them names (and male names, at that). Nevertheless, there was enough material to suggest certain structural elements that must exist. For

"I don't know how to say 'thank you' in Dothraki."

{ Daeneys Targaryen }

"There is no word for 'thank you' in Dothraki."

{ Jorah Mormont }

example, the phrase "Rakh! Rakh! Rakh haj!" is translated as "A boy! A boy! A strong boy!" I took all such translations to be canon. As such, I took this example as evidence that Dothraki lacked, at the very least, an indefinite article ("a"), that "rakh" meant "boy" and "haj" meant "strong," and

that adjectives followed nouns rather than preceded nouns.

In addition to gleaning what grammatical information I could from the texts, I also used the books to determine the sound system of the language. This was not an easy task, as George R. R. Martin makes use of a number of digraphs that could be interpreted in a number of ways, and he has stated on several different occasions that there is no "correct" way to pronounce the various names and phrases in his books—that any pronunciation the reader prefers is acceptable. My goal, then, was to come up with a way of reading the Dothraki words in the text that was both faithful to its graphic representation—so sounds spelled differently would be pronounced differently—and would sound the way most fans of the series would imagine them to sound. It was a balancing act, as some of the sounds of Dothraki are quite foreign to English, but overall I think the result is something many readers find to be both authentic and faithful to the books.

The Dothraki language, like the people, are inspired by other cultures and languages, but they are not directly related to any. The goal of a conlanger, a language creator, is to realize a linguistic system that's both unique and authentic—something that doesn't exist anywhere on Earth, but which a linguist wouldn't be surprised to find in the wild. To pull it off, a conlanger must be mindful of the patterns of existing natural languages, and of how they came to exist, but also must refrain from simply copying systems or bits of systems wholesale. To be truly authentic, a language needs its own unique history—a set of linguistic events that gave rise to the present system, irregularities and all. This is what I've attempted to do with Dothraki in order to produce a language that fits in with material from the books, but also has the wear and tear of a language that's been spoken for more than a thousand years.

Hearing the Dothraki language on-screen for the first time was one of those moments I'll remember all my life. As a conlanger, one typically works on one's languages in isolation, sharing them with other conlangers over the Internet, usually in written form or with audio files. Usually if one is hearing one's language spoken, though, it's being spoken by oneself—recorded onto an MP3 or in a YouTube video. To hear it spoken not only by total strangers but on television was . . . honestly, quite bizarre. And a lot of fun. Especially as the season progressed, and we got to hear more and more of the language, it was neat to see how each actor settled into a groove and devel-oped their own sense of what the Dothraki language was. Jason Momoa, for example, developed a distinct and consistent accent throughout the series, which I couldn't have predicted, but which, once I heard it, made sense—and worked extremely well.

DAVID BENIOFF: The actors deserve a huge amount of credit, not only for learning this tongue, but for delivering some of the season's most emotional speeches in a language only one man alive truly understands.

David Peterson's Dothraki Language Fun Facts

The name for the Dothraki people—and their language—derives from a verb meaning "to ride."

The Dothraki have four different words for "carry," three different words for "push," three different words for "pull," and at least fourteen different words for "horse," but no word that means "please."

The literal translation of the Dothraki equivalent of the English verb "to dream" is "to live a wooden life."

The words for "to fall off of," "former," "to kill," and "disgraced" all derive from the same root.

The word for "pride" is derived from the word for "braid." Grammatically, the wind is considered to be more alive than a human girl.

The Dothraki language, like Russian, doesn't distinguish between a leg and a foot, or between an arm and a hand (or, for that matter, a fingernail and a toenail).

The generic word for "good" derives from a word ultimately meaning "useful" (and "bad" from "useless").

Dothraki has more native words for horse colorings than for abstract colors (red, green, blue, and so on).

The word for "perfection" derives from the word for "stallion."

Dothraki nouns distinguish between male and female goats, horses, yaks, sheep, and mules—and humans, too—but Dothraki pronouns make no gender distinction whatsoever.

The words for "related," "weighted net," "eclipse," "dispute," "redhead," "oath," "funeral pyre," "evidence," "omen," "fang," and "harvest moon" all have one element in common: *qoy*, the Dothraki word for "blood."

JASON MOMOA: I think it elevated the character so much. And it was a lot of fun! It's like those exercises you do in acting classes where you're not allowed to speak; you can only use gibberish. It really freed me up physically, and the character emerged because of it. What I was able to do with voice, the way I changed it, those guttural sounds—I probably couldn't have found that speaking English. It was phenomenal.

DAVID J. PETERSON: As a part of the *Game of Thrones* team, I feel it's my job to add a bit of linguistic authenticity to the scenes across the Narrow Sea. In a book, one can paint a picture of the Dothraki and leave out the language, but with the medium of television nothing is left out: no costume, no sound, no suit of armor, no blade of grass. By having them speak in their own language, the show helps to ground this fantasy world in a tangible reality viewers can respond to.

D.B. WEISS: David Peterson went above and beyond the call of duty, creating a language that truly captures the feel of a culture. We look forward to the Dothraki translation of *Hamlet*, in which Claudius dies in act five, scene two.

THE BIRTH OF DRAGONS

EPISODE 110: "FIRE AND BLOOD"

THE FINAL IMAGE OF GAME OF THRONES' FIRST SEASON IS ONE OF ITS MOST DISARMING AND POWERFUL: DAENERYS TARGARYEN EMERGES UNBURNT FROM THE FLAMES OF KHAL DROGO'S SMOLDERING FUNERAL PYRE AND STANDS NAKED BEFORE HER STUNNED KHALASAR—WITH THREE NEWBORN DRAGONS WRAPPED AROUND HER, THEIR SHRIEKS ECHOING ACROSS THE DESERT LANDSCAPE, HERALDING A NEW ERA.

GEORGE R. R. MARTIN: One of the writing decisions I wrestled with was whether or not to include actual dragons. I always knew, for some reason, the Targaryens would have dragons on their banners, but were they real or was it just a symbol? I finally decided they would be real . . . and I'm glad I did.

ALAN TAYLOR (*director*): I felt lucky in season one because I got to direct two "showpieces." The first was Ned's death at the Sept of Baelor; the second was the birth of Dany's dragons. In some ways, the dragon sequence was even more satisfying because it was a very concise scene. I'd storyboarded it, and it was a real challenge because we had to shoot it at the magic hour [the last hour of sunlight] over the course of three days, basically panicking, running down from our other location,

"I will take what is mine. With fire and blood."

{ Daenerys Targaryen }

[above] *The music of dragons.* ◆ [opposite] *Concept art, the funeral pyre.* ◆ [following spread] *Daenerys walking into the fire, toward her destiny.*

grabbing two or three shots of the sequence, then running back the next day, grabbing two more shots. But it was very efficient, and it was one of the few times the storyboards didn't deviate from the finished material, which doesn't mean that's always

good. But there was something satisfying about making a plan and then going, "Wow, it worked!"

D. B. WEISS: We shot the final scene on three consecutive days in Malta, during a brief forty-five-minute window at the magic hour each day. The weather in Malta had been temperamental, and the schedule was tight. If it had rained or been too windy for one of those three days, we would not have gotten the scene, and there was no going back for reshoots. But the storm gods were kind, and Emilia and Iain were perfect one- or two-take wonders.

MICHELE CLAPTON: It was very important to me that Dany wear her wedding dress from the very first episode—that she walk into the pyre with it and have it burn along with Drogo.

ALAN TAYLOR: In the book, it's actually a nighttime scene, and there's a beautiful line in both the script and the book, actually the last line: "The night came alive with the music of dragons." But from the beginning, I was thinking we were going to want to hear the dragons' voices echoing over the landscape, and I wanted the audience to be able to sense the feel of the landscape. Also, I liked the idea of saying at the close of the first season that this is the dawn of a new world. So we changed it to morning. Hopefully the fans weren't too upset!

DAVID BENIOFF: The dragons themselves were the most vital effect on the season one VFX calendar. We started with the concept art, and we consulted George because he's been thinking for twenty years about how he wanted the dragons to look: two legs, not four, and articulated claws at the tips of their wings. After the concept paintings were approved, the artists built a maquette—a life-size model of the baby dragon, which can then be scanned into the computers and used by the CGI team as they built more lifelike dragons. If the drag-

EMILIA CLARKE: **That was my favorite scene of all, obviously — after her baby dies, Dany is forced to kill Drogo, burn him on the pyre, and become the Mother of Dragons. Emotionally she's walking into that fire to be reborn. It's the defining moment of her life. The moment she truly stops being a child and becomes a woman. It's the basis for everything that happens afterward: "They've taken everything from me. They're not taking my dragons."**

ons looked fake, the entire scene would fall apart. The sequence would become silly instead of momentous, laughable instead of moving. So thank you, thank you, thank you to everyone involved in creating those dragons. The VFX team suffered through months of our nitpicky notes and succeeded beyond our expectations.

ALAN TAYLOR: We wanted them to feel like unsteady newborn babies, the way a foal takes its first steps, and the way the VFX team captured that, with the dragon on Dany's shoulder, opening its wings for the first time . . . they did a helluva job. And that close-up on Emilia's face when she looks up—whew! And Iain as well, when he says, "Blood of my blood." It's

good to have convincing dragons and good to have a wide shot with this vast desert, but in the end, the scene is built around those two close-ups. They're reacting the way we'd react if we encountered something this extraordinary.

It's funny. Watching season two unfurl, I was naive. I thought, "Oh, she's got dragons now. Cut to: they're flying through the sky scorching the earth." No, they're newborn creatures, they're unsteady, they're fragile—who knows if they're going to make it? It takes them years to grow up. At first you think she's going to become Joan of Arc with flamethrowers, but you get to season two, and she's wandering the Red Waste, certain death in every direction, and you realize, "Oh wait, she's screwed!" ❧

QARTH & THE RED WASTE

D. B. WEISS *(executive producer, writer)*: In this story, the greatest power and the greatest dangers in the world often seem to lie on its margins. A perfect example is the city of Qarth, where Daenerys spends the bulk of the second season. With the exception of the spectacular city gates, which Gemma Jackson designed and Rainer Gombos and the rest of the season two VFX team augmented, Qarth was shot on real locations in Dubrovnik, Croatia, which were retrofitted by the design team.

EMILIA CLARKE *(Daenerys Targaryen)*: In season two, when Dany finds herself in Qarth, it's almost like she's in King's Landing. It's a more political world, which she's not used to. She's gone from having this epic change and this fast-paced adventure, and she's essentially thrown into a waiting room. She's very frustrated. She has these creatures, these dragons, but they're not grown yet, and her journey has stalled. I think, this season, you're really seeing that she's a woman. She may look like a girl with a ragged band, but it's a quest for her to be taken seriously and treated as an individual. "I am a woman. I am going to be queen." ❧

GEMMA JACKSON: There's a great deal of beautiful Italianate architecture in Dubrovnik, which we used for the various sets in Qarth. The palace of Xaro Xhoan Daxos [Dany's wealthy patron] is an old monastery on Lokrum island. But, again, we're not sticking to one style here; the gates and surrounding walls have a Turkish quality to them.

[opposite top and above] *At the start of season two, Dany is forced to lead her ragged khalasar into the arid and desolate Red Waste.* ♦ [above] *Qarth concept art.* ♦ [left] *A meeting of the Thirteen.*

COSTUMING QARTH

MICHELE CLAPTON: The Qartheen were a lot of fun to do. Like King's Landing, it's a port city, but it's also very exotic, opulent, and mysterious. Dany finds herself there and it's so far removed from any other place she's been before. We were able to take some risks with it.

[opposite top] *Dany in Qarth.* ◆ [opposite middle] *Daenerys' wealthy Qartheen patron Xaro Xhoan Daxos (played by Nonso Anozie).* ◆ [opposite bottom] *Dany and her handmaidens, Doreah (Roxanne McKee) and Irri (Amrita Acharia), neither of whom will leave Qarth alive.* ◆ [left] *Ian Hanmore as Pyat Pree, a warlock of Qarth and adversary of Dany in season two.* [above] *Laura Pradelska as Quaithe.* ◆ [below] *Costume concept drawings, Qartheen citizens.*

BEHIND THE SCENES
AT *GAME OF THRONES*

[top left] *"Final checks!"* ♦ [top middle] *Weapons master Tommy Dunne.* ♦ [top right] *Owen Teale (Alliser Thorne), Peter Vaughan (Maester Aemon), and James Cosmo (Lord Commander Mormont) keep dry.* ♦ [middle left] *Getting that trail of blood juuust right.* ♦ [middle] *A special rig is used for the skewering of Ser Hugh, in the tourney episode from season one.* ♦ [middle right] *Getting that fatal neck wound, juuuust right.* ♦ [bottom left] *King Joffrey and his crossbow—it's good to be the king.* ♦ [bottom right] *Director Alan Taylor blocks out a scene with Maisie Williams.*

[top left] *One of season two's directors of photography, Martin Kenzie.* ♦ [top middle] *Production designer Gemma Jackson.* ♦ [top right] *George R. R. Martin chats up Peter Dinklage on the Eyrie set in Belfast.* ♦ [middle left] *The severed heads are ready for their close-ups.* ♦ [middle] *Making sure the blood spatter matches the previous day's footage.* ♦ [middle right] *The sign says it all.* ♦ [bottom right] *Shooting Bran's fateful "accident."* ♦ [bottom middle] *Khals Benioff and Drogo.* ♦ [bottom right] *Season two director David Petrarca and some Lannister corpses.*

[top left] *Shooting the battle of the Blackwater.* ♦ [top middle] *A very brave stunt performer shoots Pyat Pree's final moments.* ♦ [top right] *The Stark boys on the Winterfell set . . . in happier times.* ♦ [middle left] *Season one director Tim Van Patten and Sean Bean.* ♦ [bottom left] *Maisie Williams (Arya) and Miltos Yerolemou (Syrio) sharing a light-hearted moment.* ♦ [bottom right] *On set with the king and his "dog."*

[top left] *Shooting in the throne room, at the Paint Hall in Belfast.* ♦ [top right] *Another casualty on the GoT set.* ♦
[middle left] *Touching Emilia up on set in Croatia.* ♦ [Middle] *Stay warm, Sophie!* ♦ [bottom left] *Touching the green screen up on set in Northern Ireland.* ♦ [bottom right] *Harry Lloyd and Emilia Clarke practice the choke-hold between takes—sibling abuse can be fun!*

A GAME OF PRANKS

Making a weekly drama series on an epic scale is a pressure-packed, extremely serious business indeed, but there is room for fun as well. The first of what was destined to become an annual tradition started during the production of season one, when David Benioff and Dan Weiss decided to see just how closely the actors were reading the scripts. . . .

· Kit Harington ·

DAVID BENIOFF *(executive producer, writer)*: You may not have noticed this, but in addition to being a talented actor, Kit Harington is a good-looking guy. We assumed that, like most good-looking guys, he likes being a good-looking guy. So while we were shooting the first season, when we distributed new drafts of Episode 108, we gave Kit a copy with these Jon Snow scenes in place of the actual scenes.

D. B. WEISS *(executive producer, writer)*: When Kit came to the set after having read it, we told him that HBO was worried the Jon Snow story line was too Harry Potter, and they wanted to do something to make it darker. They thought he was such a strong actor that he could handle it, etc. We kept this up until we started laughing. He was a remarkably good sport about the whole thing. I think he had actually resigned himself to possibly spending years and years on the show with no hair and no upper lip.

GAME OF THRONES - "Episode VIII" - FULL WHITE - 7/30/10 23.
25   CONTINUED: 25

Othor's severed arm comes racing from the shadows, quick as spider, and grabs for Mormont's legs.

Jon kicks the arm away, grabs the lamp from the Old Bear's hand, throws it at the tangle of drapes on the floor.

Glass shatters, spreading the lamp oil. The flames spread, and the drapes go up with a great WHOOSH.

                    JON
              Ghost! To me!

Jon plunges his hand into the fire, seizes the burning drapes, and FLINGS them at the dead man, engulfing them both in flame.

As the wight staggers and spins, burning, Jon hustles the Old Bear from the solar.

INT. MORMONT'S OUTER CHAMBER - CONTINUOUS

Mormont wraps Jon in his own cloak to extinguish the flames ravaging the young man.

When the fire is finally out, we see by torchlight that all of Jon's hair has been burnt down to the scalp.

The skin on the top half of his face has been melted in the extreme heat, blistered and pustulant.

Despite what must be the extreme agony of permanent disfigurement, Jon stands stoically by his master's side.

Mormont eyes the mutilated boy with amazement at the lad's courage.

Jon's upper lip is completely gone, exposing the top row of his teeth.

                    JON
              Are you all right, Lord Commander?

                    MORMONT
              Gods, boy. I was wrong about you.
              You're a ranger, through and
              through.

Jon smiles, his teeth shining brightly in his destroyed face.

Mormont, sickened, has to look away.

· Alfie Allen ·

D. B. WEISS: It became very clear very early on that Alfie Allen's performance as Theon Greyjoy in season two was going to be a standout. We would tell him this all the time—"You are kicking ass out there," etc.—but he was still worried about the state of his role. Would he be coming back in season three? He wasn't in book three. Were we just going to kill him?

We didn't say. Eventually, we sent him this scene:

```
GAME OF THRONES - "Episode 210" - FULL WHITE        9.7.11


    Infected with battle lust, none of the Ironborn notice HODOR
    emerging from the shadows outside of the crypt entrance. BRAN
    sits in his customary saddle on the giant's back.

                    THEON
            Mothers will name their sons for
            us!

                    IRONBORN
            Aye!

                    THEON
            Girls will think of us with their
            lovers inside them, will whisper
            our names as they cum!

                    IRONBORN
            Aye!

    AHoooooooooooooo.

                    THEON
            And whoever kills that fucking horn
            blower will stand in bronze above
            the shores of Pyke!

                    IRONBORN
            Aye!

    Hodor creeps closer to the Ironborn, staying to the shadows,
    unseen by all.

    Bran draws a small dagger from a sheath at his belt.

                    THEON
            (thumping his chest)
            What is dead may never die!

                    IRONBORN
            What is dead may never die!

                    BRAN
            (whisper in Hodor's ear)
            Now.

    Hodor charges forward. Theon's back is to him. He doesn't
    hear them coming -- only sees the faces of the Ironborn as
    they begin to react.

    Theon turns, mouth opening.

                    BRAN
            For Winterfell!

    He plunges his dagger deep into Theon's chest.

    Theon's eyes widen and he sinks to his knees.
```

```
GAME OF THRONES - "Episode 210" - FULL WHITE        9.7.11
CONTINUED:

    Dagmer raises his spear -- and an arrow sprouts from his eye
    socket.

    OSHA stands in the shadows near the crypt entrance, bow in
    hand. She looses another arrow and fells another Ironborn.

                    BRAN
            Run, Hodor, run!

                    HODOR
            Hodor! Hodor!

    Hodor runs for the gates. The surviving Ironborn chase after
    them -- until they hear a monstrous growling behind them.
    They turn to see two direwolves loping their way.

    SUMMER and SHAGGYDOG pounce on the Ironborn and devour them.

    Theon, still on his knees, blood pouring from the dagger
    still protruding from his chest, stares in disbelief as his
    conquest comes undone. All those dreams of empire, crumbling
    to the dust.

    Osha approaches him, bow in hand, arrow knocked. (N.B., the
    exact same position Theon was in when he captured Osha in
    Episode 106.)

    Theon coughs and blood pours from his mouth. He manages a
    small smile, the last smile of his life, as Hodor turns and
    walks back with Bran on his back.

    Bran looks down at Theon. Theon looks up at Bran.

                    THEON
            I'm glad you're alive.

                    BRAN
            I'm glad you're dead.

    Theon collapses face forward into the dust.

                    OSHA
            (to Bran )
            Time to go North. It's not safe
            here anymore.

                    BRAN
            (re: Theon)
            Should we bury him?

                    OSHA
            Leave him for the wolves. They
            haven't eaten in days.

    Summer and Shaggydog lick their lips and stare down at their
    dinner in the dust.
```

DAVID BENIOFF: We didn't hear from Alfie for two weeks. Finally, we called him. He was on holiday in Ibiza, on a sailboat. He said he was fine with it. He thought it was a good way to go. We asked him if he'd consider coming back as a zombie, which sometimes happens to people in this show. After a long silence on the line, he said he'd consider it. "It would mean having no dialogue and being naked most of the time," we said, "but it would still be acting."

He drew the line at naked zombie. So we told him there was no way we were killing him off.

EPILOGUE:

REFLECTIONS ON GAME OF THRONES

D.B. WEISS *(executive producer, writer)*: It's a fantasy show. We love that it's a fantasy show. When people work in a genre and then bend themselves into pretzels to deny it and disavow the genre they're working in, to me that says more about them than the genre in question.

So this is a fantasy show, and at the heart of this particular fantasy show, you've got people whose situations and motivations are, I hope, familiar and recognizable to everyone: They love someone who doesn't love them back. Two people they love are asking mutually exclusive things of them. They're desperate to be respected and taken seriously. They want to protect their families but aren't sure how. They're in over their heads but are too proud or afraid to admit it. They want more money. They want to get laid. If characters are tapping into this universal bedrock, it doesn't matter whether they're carrying swords or guns or briefcases.

JOHN BRADLEY *(Samwell Tarly)*: There's an absolute credible humanity about it. These people could literally be anywhere.

You can see people having the same quandaries in life that everyone has, albeit on a huge scale. It's like Shakespeare—you can be in huge, outrageous places and situations, but it comes down to a deep-rooted understanding of psychology and human situations. The fantasy elements are treated seriously by the characters. If you do believe in the characters, as people and families with psychologically valid relationships, to have something otherworldly like the White Walkers as a presence is all the more terrifying. You think, "How terrifying would it be to have to face these things!" But you have

to believe in the characters first for that to have any weight. I think it's a testament to the performances, particularly the Starks. You genuinely believe they are a family.

SEAN BEAN *(Ned Stark)*: I suppose it's a grown-up fantasy. The violence, the brutality, and of course all these interesting characters. I don't know how George invented all of these characters—it's unlike anything I've worked on before. And it's a courageous thing to undertake for HBO. It's been great working with them because you can do what you want.

IAIN GLEN *(Jorah Mormont)*: Unlike stories of a similar ilk, *Game of Thrones* portrays a savage and cruel reality, rife with political and psychological intrigue. It's definitely for grown-ups. The "fantasy" is only lightly touched upon—a supernatural presence that is presumed by the people and becomes manifest in varying ways as the story unfolds. Perhaps newcomers have been surprised by the intricacy and richness of the material and how much they enjoy it. Notwithstanding the cost of trying to bring the epic scope of George R. R. Martin's world to life, television as a vehicle has virtues that can offer potent visceral immediacy, if it is well executed. And I hope and believe that HBO and all the creative team have done the novels proud.

FRANK DOELGER (*producer*): I think there were some reservations early on that this show would be dismissed by a mass audience as "genre." The more I thought about it, it's the kind of show HBO would do because no one else would. I think the thing that was most surprising for me were the numbers of calls I got after Ned's execution. I realized that people were so invested in the characters, and therefore invested in the show, that it was truly shocking to them. To me, it was a sign that we'd done our jobs, creating fascinating real characters, and it was no longer a genre piece at all. It was a great drama about great characters that had fantastical, imaginative elements. As much as people enjoyed the dragons and the direwolves, in the feedback I've gotten, people keep coming back to a handful of scenes, none of which have anything to do with the fantasy elements. And that's what I think seems to have touched everybody.

LENA HEADEY (*Cersei Lannister*): I think it's fun in that it's five shows in one. The audience appreciates that—it's an exciting, versatile show. And the characters never stop moving, growing, changing. No one ever remains what you think they are. That makes it so exciting. Visually, it's so incredible and cinematic. And David and Dan love it and care about what they're doing. So when we as actors get ahold of it, we feel the same. I think people see that. I think they relate to the theme of family. After all, we've all got family that we slightly love and slightly don't.

CONLETH HILL (*Varys*): I think the show is a tremendously good human-interest story, and there are so many humans to be interested in. There's something for every-

body. The game playing that goes on in the show goes on all the time and has throughout history, but it's left out of the history books, isn't it? Only the facts are written down, but the maneuvering it took to get there is left out. That's the element I find most fascinating about it.

ALAN TAYLOR (*director*): There's something about our time in which these modes of mythology seem to be catching on.

Maybe it's a combination of escapism and that they speak to what we're worried about. There's a lot of the stuff in *Game of Thrones*—the idea of imminent destruction, the fact that there's war, there's this anxiety of the world—that we share. George's basic idea, I think, was to do fantasy but with a mind-set that's very much like our own, so the attitude toward magic is ours. It used to be in the world, but it's not anymore. They think of themselves as being "modern" people in a dark, troubling, screwed-up time, just as we do. We'll see if the appetite for it continues.

EMILIA CLARKE (*Daenerys Targaryen*): There's a beautifully healthy mix of incredible plot and rounded characters. I always say, if you take the essence of *Game of Thrones* out of the fantasy genre, it still stands up as an incredible piece. You're invested in these people. But with the fantasy elements on top, it's terrific because anything is possible. We all have imaginations and love to have them indulged.

KIT HARINGTON (*Jon Snow*): I think these days, there is a lot of fantasy-based stuff coming out, and that says something about the state of the world at the moment. People are looking for escapism. What I

love about this series—and the way HBO is doing it—is that it's very gritty, based in reality. It's not pure escapism. It deals with some hard emotions and horrible things.

LIAM CUNNINGHAM (*Davos Seaworth*): I think it's glorious in that it doesn't patronize the audience; it celebrates their intelligence. It's funny—everyone I talked to, when they heard I was cast, their initial reaction was physical. They grabbed your arm: "You're doing *Game of Thrones!*" I think for most of them, it starts off as a guilty pleasure—"All right, fine, I'll have a look." Then they watch the first episode and see what a mountain it is to climb, as a viewer. Then they get to episode two and they're hooked! Then by the time they're at the end, it's, "No. God, no! Not Ned!" It's compulsory viewing. You have to watch it. How many shows can you say that about these days?

GWENDOLINE CHRISTIE (*Brienne of Tarth*): I think it transcends the regular fantasy genre by giving us relationships that are as human as they are fantastic. We see characters dealing with death, prejudice,

violence, love, politics, and unerring quests for power, all within an enthralling and "other" realm. It is perhaps the established "otherness" of this world that engages us, the audience. We are gripped by and identify so fully with these very human themes that form the foundation of our lives and are simultaneously captivated by the beauty and strangeness of a world that includes dwarfs, giants, knights, queens, and dragons—all the things that thrilled us as children.

RICHARD MADDEN (*Robb Stark*): At the end of the day, it's about people making

choices. Sometimes right, sometimes wrong, and I think people enjoy watching the consequences of all these decisions. It's kind of an exaggerated version of our world, of how we live day to day.

DAVID BENIOFF (*executive producer, writer*): I fell in love with the books, even though I hadn't gone near a "fantasy" novel in twenty years. But I didn't fall in love with the magic, even though the magical elements happen to be a lot of fun. I fell in love with the characters. With Arya Stark and Jon Snow and Theon Greyjoy and Tyrion Lannister and Daenerys Targaryen and Sansa and Bran and Jorah and Cersei and Jaime and Robb and Samwell and—you see what I mean? Has any book series ever introduced so many memorable characters into the world? Well, we hope to do the same with our series. We're going to make viewers all over the world fall in love with these characters. And then we're going to kill them. The characters, I mean. Not the viewers. We haven't figured out how to do that yet.

PETER DINKLAGE (*Tyrion Lannister*): *Game of Thrones* is great storytelling. It crosses genres. I actually don't see it as a genre piece anymore. These characters are as vibrant and real as anything I have come

across in more traditional great fiction. I think it is narrow-minded to put things into separate categories or dismiss them for being in the far corner of your local bookstore. George R. R. Martin created complex, unforgettable, extremely realistic characters. People seem to think that HBO took a risk. I wish more of us did.

BRYAN COGMAN is executive story editor on *Game of Thrones* and has written two episodes of the series. When not in Belfast shooting the show, he lives with his wife and daughter in Los Angeles, California.

DAVID BENIOFF's latest novel is *City of Thieves*. He is co-creator and executive producer of the Emmy-nominated HBO series *Game of Thrones*. He lives in Los Angeles with his wife and two daughters.

D. B. WEISS is the author of *Lucky Wander Boy*, and has worked on numerous film projects such as *Halo*, *Ender's Game*, and *The Game*. Dan co-created and is an executive producer of the Emmy-nominated *Game of Thrones* for HBO. He lives in Los Angeles with his wife and two sons.

GEORGE R. R. MARTIN is an award-winning writer of books and screenplays, including the bestselling fantasy series *A Song of Ice and Fire*. He lives in Santa Fe, New Mexico, with his wife.